The 'gift' of a chi
When should th
Service be used?
Naming ceremon

Baptism

What does baptism do?
What do the promises require?
What do parents seek for their children?
Naming in the Baptism Service
Parenting in the Baptism Service

A three or four-fold service?
Marriage and Services of Prayer and Dedication
Services of Prayer and Dedication after a Civil Marriage

Bibliography	173
Appendix 1	179
Answers to Exercise at end of Chapter 4	183
Index	
Biblical References	186
Names	190
Subject	192

Introduction

This book is a collaboration between Imogen Clout, a family lawyer, who is also an Anglican Reader, and John Rogerson, a (retired) professor of Biblical Studies, who is also an Anglican priest.

It came about because Imogen was working on an update of a leaflet on parental law published on the web. At that time, in 2010, a number of new measures had crept onto the statute book and as a result, the ways in which people could legally become parents, or acquire Parental Responsibility, had changed. The law had become more complex. She realised that many lawyers had not yet made sense of all the changes, neither had the general public, or the media. It was also likely that the Church had not thought about what these changes entailed, and whether language and forms of liturgy would need adaptation. She shared her concerns with a small group convened by John, which meets regularly to discuss theological and scriptural matters. John had already been working on a consideration of biblical teaching on the family, and its application to modern life. A collaboration was born.

For both of us it is crucial that churches should practise active hospitality; it is an essential part of our Christian life as the body of Christ. Churches therefore need to examine their liturgies, and the language they use, as well as their general approach and policies, to make sure that they are welcoming, not by default but by design. This book is intended both for church ministers and their lay congregations, to inform their

More Places at the Table:

Legal and biblical perspectives on modern family life

J. W Rogerson
&
Imogen Clout

Published in 2013 by FeedARead.com Publishing
– Arts Council funded

Copyright © J.W. Rogerson and Imogen Clout

The author or authors assert their moral right under the Copyright, Designs and Patents Act, 1988, to be identified as the author or authors of this work.

All Rights reserved. No part of this publication may be reproduced, copied, stored in a retrieval system, or transmitted, in any form or by any means, without the prior written consent of the copyright holder, nor be otherwise circulated in any form of binding or cover other than that in which it is published and without a similar condition being imposed on the subsequent purchaser.

A CIP catalogue record for this title is available from the British Library.

About the authors

John Rogerson is Emeritus Professor of Biblical Studies, University of Sheffield, and an Emeritus Canon of Sheffield Cathedral. An Old Testament scholar, his publications cover the history, geography, theology and sociology of the Old Testament, as well as the history of biblical interpretation. He has also published in the field of biblical ethics, and the use of the Bible in social, moral and political questions. An Anglican priest of many years' standing, he is active in ministry at Beauchief Abbey in Sheffield.

He has been married to Rosalind for forty-eight years.

Imogen Clout worked for many years as a family solicitor, lecturer and, latterly, family mediator. She is the author of books on family law including The Which? Guide to Divorce and the Which? Guide to Living Together, and also materials published on the web.

She is an Anglican Reader and also a Methodist member of her church, which is a joint Anglican/Methodist partnership, with a fully integrated congregation. She has served as the Sheffield Diocese Lay Development Officer.

She is married and has three (nearly grown-up) children. She lives in Sheffield.

Thanks and acknowledgements

The authors wish to thank the numerous people whom they have involved in the discussions that informed this book, particularly the Bible and Society Group and informal meetings of clergy and lay people in Sheffield, and the Anglican Diocese of Sheffield.

Thanks are also due to
- Jony Serina Raj Sodadasi, who gave us invaluable help with the indexes.
- Father Michael Clothier of Downside Abbey for some insights into the Roman Catholic position on family life

The prayer on page 146 from A New Zealand Prayer Book is © The General Synod of the Anglican Church of Canada, 1985. Used with permission.

The address to the baptismal candidate(s) on page 162 is © Uniting Church of Australia. Used with permission.

Extracts from *Common Worship: Services and Prayers* are copyright © The Archbishops' Council, 2000, and are reproduced by permission. All rights reserved. copyright@churchofengland.org

Extracts from *The Alternative Service* Book are copyright © Archbishops' Council, 1980. Used by permission. All rights reserved. copyright@churchofengland.org

Contents

	Page
Introduction	8
Chapter 1 **Parental Responsibility and its Implications**	11
Chapter 2 **How you become a parent**	23

What the law says about becoming a parent
Legal parenthood
Parental Responsibility
How does the law work in practice?
    Mothers
    Married male/female couple
    Civil partners
        Lesbian civil partners
        Gay civil partners
        If a civil partnership is dissolved
    Unmarried couples
        Male/female
        Unmarried couples – lesbian
        Unmarried couples – gay
        A single parent
    Step and other relationships
    Other people looking after children

Chapter 3   41
The legal position of couples
Marriage
Civil partnerships
Cohabiting couples
Terminology and reality
Marriage and tradition

Chapter 4 53
What does the Bible say?
Using the Bible – Old Testament precedents
New Testament teachings
Biblical family structures
What does the Bible say about parenting?

Chapter 5 73
Families, the law and the Church
False nostalgia
What is a 'Christian family?'
Historical perspective
A modern change in legal sensibility

Chapter 6 96
Christian family practice
Early Christian communities
The development of a theology of Christian marriage
Godparents
The Continental Reformers
Richard Baxter's position
Karl Barth's contribution to the discussion

Chapter 7 122
Some Suggestions for Today from the Bible and its Use
Precept or example?
Structures of grace
Looking at the quality of relationships

Chapter 8 134
More Places at the Table: liturgies, their strengths and weaknesses
What is litugy for?
The Churching of Women
Thanksgiving for the Gift of a Child

discussions, and provoke active consideration of how such welcome may be achieved.

We found that there is a tendency for churches to behave as though the only valid family model is one of a mother, a father, and two children. This tidy image, which seems to come from the 1950s, is not only unlike modern reality, but is completely different from the family patterns that prevailed in earlier times. We also found that the Bible offers very little precedent for such a narrow picture of family life. Somehow we need to free ourselves from the constraint of our 1950s time-warp.

One of our chief concerns is for children who are brought up in what the Church might regard as an 'irregular' family arrangement. They are of course blameless (if blame is to be attributed at all) for the lives of the adults who bring them up. If they encounter Church practices that imply that their families are in some way 'wrong', they are likely to feel rejected, and even excluded. And parents too, whatever judgement people might like to make about their relationship with each other, need help and support to bring up their children in a loving and stable environment. Hitherto, it seems to us that parents have not had much acknowledgement of their role, as far as the Church is concerned

There are few prayers in our liturgy that recognise that parenthood can be difficult and stressful, as well as a joy and a privilege. We feel that churches should support and encourage this and liturgies should make a point of offering prayer and comfort for parents.

We have written this book to set out both the legal and historical position of families and the biblical perspectives that need to be taken into account. It has been suggested to us that perhaps the detailed legal information is unnecessary, but it seems clear to us that in the recent debates on same-sex marriage, much of the discussion is marred by a poor understanding of what the law really is, and what the Bible really contains. Having said which, you may feel that you can skip through some of the technicalities. They are there if you need to understand a particular family arrangement and the implications it might have for its members.

Given the sensitivity of the topics discussed in this book, it is bound to be controversial. We have not sought to make it controversial, however, but to explain and to inform readers about what is the case. The matters dealt with are too important to be debated in the light of ignorance or misinformation.

We believe that the quality of human relationships is more important than whether or not they conform to traditional models, and we believe that anyone seeking the support of churches should be welcomed with graciousness and love.

Sheffield
August 2013

Chapter 1

Parental Responsibility and its Implications

by Imogen Clout

The effects of the Children Act 1989, the concepts of Parental Responsibility, contact and residence.

1989, as those who lived through it will remember, was a momentous year of change. The spectre of the Cold War that had overshadowed the youth of the baby-boomer generation crumbled and faded. There are abiding images from that year: of Wenceslas Square in Prague filled with crowds, and the Berlin Wall falling to rubble under people's hands. And during that momentous year of change the Children Act slid (comparatively quietly) onto the statute books in this country[1]. The changes it brought about in English law[2] were equally radical, if less dramatic, compared with

---

[1] It received the Royal Assent on 16th November 1989.
[2] Any reference to English law in this work means the law in the jurisdictional area of England and Wales. Scotland and Northern Ireland have separate jurisdictions, and family law is not always the same.

the other changes taking place in the world that year. They were to set the stage for other changes in family law, in particular the role of parents and the way their relationship with their children is expressed in law. It also changed the way that the law dealt with children who needed to be taken from their parents for their own protection[3]. Lawyers call this Public Law. It takes up the larger part of the Act, but is not the focus of this chapter which concentrates on what lawyers call Private Law: the law about the legal relationship of parents and children in families.

The Children Act 1989 was heavily influenced by the recommendations of the Law Commission's 1988 Report on *Guardianship and Custody*. This recommended the adoption of the term 'Parental Responsibility' to replace the idea of parental rights, as it 'would reflect the everyday reality of being a parent and emphasise the responsibilities of all who are in that position.' It stated that 'such a change would make little difference in substance'. While technically that statement was accurate – since the Act did not change the 'bundle of rights and duties' that make up the legal concept of parenthood - we would argue that the Children Act did bring about a change in the way in which lawyers would be able to speak about the law to their clients and how people would therefore think about their roles as parents.

---

[3] These are generally referred to as care proceedings, though children are no longer described as being 'in care', but (confusingly) as 'looked-after children'.

This change, from rights to responsibilities, is a subtle change, but a powerful one. Legal language does affect the way people *feel* about the law. A parent who comes to a lawyer demanding what he or she sees as his or her *rights* over a child finds that the experienced family lawyer will not conceptualise the legal issues in that way. Instead, the good lawyer will speak of Parental Responsibility, (with some emphasis on the latter word) and explain that this is something that can be shared, or exercised individually. If parents are sharing it, there is an expectation in law that they will, as far as possible do this cooperatively, and the welfare of the child is the over-riding principle. Effectively, it is the child who has rights – if the language of rights is to be used at all. The Act did create a shift, and a welcome one, away from the chattel and property language which was the legacy of the common law.

In practical terms the Children Act had no immediate impact; it would be 1991 before the various provisions started to come into effect. Overnight from 14th October 1991 lawyers and their clients had to start to deal with new legal terms and new legal concepts. The Act abandoned the old concepts and terms of 'custody' and 'joint custody', 'care and control' and 'access'. Instead, it introduced new legal terms and concepts: 'parental responsibility', 'residence', and 'contact'. Some twenty years later the media still continue to use the old terms, assuming that they mean the same thing. They are wrong to do so. The changes were not cosmetic. The Children Act created a new legal framework, intended to change the way people thought about parenthood and the way it fitted into the law.

'Parental Responsibility' now has a precise legal meaning. It is not capitalised in the Act, but we will use capitals in this book to indicate where we are using it in its legal sense. Parental Responsibility is defined in section 3 of the Act as *'all the rights, duties, powers, responsibilities and authority which by law a parent of a child has in relation to a child and his[4] property.'* To non-lawyers, this is not, of course, particularly helpful as a definition, because the Act does not spell out what those rights and duties are. To find those out, you have to go back to the common law – the body of precedent and legal authority that has built up over centuries.

It is worth bearing in mind that English common law is fundamentally rooted in property law, and for many centuries children, like wives, were treated more like property than people. Historically, therefore, the list of 'rights' has outweighed the list of 'duties', and children have been seen (legally) as part of the assets of the family and important because they will continue the property-owning family line.

There is no definitive common law or statutory list of parental rights and duties, and most of them are not absolute rights or duties, but modified by legislation and by case law. The list of rights would generally include the right to:

---

[4] As in all legislation, the male is assumed to include the female unless otherwise stated.

- consent to medical treatment for a child[5]
- consent to the child's adoption
- consent to the child's marriage (if the child was under 18)
- choose or change the child's surname
- choose the child's religion
- choose the child's education
- manage the child's property
- discipline the child (within the constraints of the law).

Duties would generally include the duty to:
- house the child
- maintain the child financially
- care for and protect the child
- nurture the child and not neglect him/her
- educate the child according to legal requirements.

These are not exhaustive lists: there are other rights and duties, some of which seem rather outmoded. For instance, traditionally a parent has had the 'right' to a child's 'services'. That is, you can make your child work for you, which had perhaps more relevance in a time when you could send your child up a chimney or out to a factory.

---

[5] though this has a recent modification by the Gillick principle (named after the test case brought by Mrs Victoria Gillick: *"As a matter of Law the parental right to determine whether or not their minor child below the age of sixteen will have medical treatment terminates if and when the child achieves sufficient understanding and intelligence to understand fully what is proposed."* Lord Scarman. Gillick v West Norfolk and Wisbech AHA. 1986 HL

Today, parents may count themselves lucky if their child makes the bed or sets the table without protest.

Though the Children Act did not create new rights and duties, it changed the way these are treated in law. Divorce does not extinguish Parental Responsibility; both parents continue to have an equal status in relation to their children[6]. This was not the case before the Act; after divorce it was possible for one parent to be awarded 'custody, care and control', though orders for 'joint custody' were becoming more common by the time the Act was passed. Parental Responsibility can also be acquired[7] by people who are not by blood a child's parents. It can also be shared by more than two people, if they all have a parental role for a child. We will look at the way that it can be acquired or conferred later in this chapter.

The Act signalled the change of emphasis that it was intended to bring about in its first section, which sets out that the child's welfare is to be the 'paramount consideration' of the court in any question about the child's upbringing or the administration of the child's property. Section 1 includes what has been called the 'welfare checklist' of factors the court must consider:

---

[6] Married parents are treated differently to unmarried parents. See Chapter 2

[7] 'Acquire' is the lawyers' verb for 'getting' Parental Responsibility. It conveys a rather unfortunate metaphor, as though Parental Responsibility is a commodity to be bought or sold.

(a) the ascertainable wishes and feelings of the child concerned (considered in the light of his[8] age and understanding);
(b) his physical, emotional and educational needs;
(c) the likely effect on him of any change in his circumstances;
(d) his age, sex, background and any characteristics of his which the court considers relevant;
(e) any harm which he has suffered or is at risk of suffering;
(f) how capable each of his parents, and any other person in relation to whom the court considers the question to be relevant, is of meeting his needs.

It perhaps needs stating, for the avoidance of doubt, and to counter some of the misleading statements that you may encounter in the media, that there is absolutely no bias in the Act in favour of the mother or the father. The Act is completely silent about whether one parent or the other is to be preferred as a child's main carer. Nor does the Act state anywhere what sort or amount of 'contact' is to be treated as normative.[9] If a case comes before a court to be decided, the appropriateness of each parent as carer will be considered by the court. There is no judicial authority or precedent to say that mothers are to be preferred over fathers. Each case is decided on its own facts using the welfare checklist in the Act.

---

[8] See footnote 4.

[9] Pressure groups such as Fathers 4 Justice, who tend to couch their critique in terms of 'fairness' have campaigned for a statutory norm for shared residence.

The Act also introduced the 'no order' principle. This, too, is in section 1:

(5) Where a court is considering whether or not to make one or more orders under this Act with respect to a child, it shall not make the order or any of the orders <u>unless it considers that doing so would be better for the child than making no order at all.</u> (our emphasis.)

This 'hands-off' approach was a very significant change. The implication was that as far as possible parents should take responsibility for making arrangements for their children, and were the people best qualified to do so. The court should always be seen as the last resort.

For most parents who are splitting up, this approach is a sensible one, as the vast majority are able to agree fair arrangements for their children without too much long-term hostility. This may come as a surprise, as it is not the impression that the media generally convey[10]. Only a small proportion of couples will have a serious wrangle over arrangements and an even smaller proportion will end up taking that issue to court. Even at court, the procedure is designed so that as far as possible there is scope for settling the case before if goes all the way to a final hearing.

However there are some couples who would be more comfortable (they feel) with the law telling them what to do. This puts a heavy burden of responsibility on family lawyers, since it is their advice, and approach to these cases, which is highly influential. In the last few years family law, which relies heavily on legal aid for funding,

---

[10] Happy families are not generally good copy.

has become less and less remunerative, with the result that many skilled lawyers have given it up, and it is often handled by young, inexperienced lawyers and para-legals. Rather late in the day, changes are being introduced that attempt to steer all divorcing couples towards the possibility of mediation. And couples who end up in court over children's matters can be sent by the judge to attend a Parenting Information Programme. These courses, based very much on American models, help parents to focus on their children's needs and can be very helpful in resolving conflict. Unfortunately they are not at present available to parents who have not issued proceedings at court.

For family lawyers, one of the most significant effects of the changes introduced by the Children Act was the way that the courts were now to deal with parents who were divorcing. Before the Act parents were expected to attend the divorce court on the day that their Decree Nisi was granted, to explain to a judge what arrangements were being made for the children after the divorce. The judge would want to know from the Petitioner (the person seeking the divorce) which parent the children would live with and whether any arrangements for 'access' had been agreed. Provided the parents had agreed the arrangements the judge would then make an order for 'custody' or 'joint custody': this said whether one or both parents was to have the power to make decisions for the child's future; 'care and control': whom the child lived with and who would therefore make the day to day decisions about the child's welfare and nurture; and 'access': how the non-resident parent was to see the child. Access was often just ordered as 'reasonable access', which was on the basis that the parents could work it out reasonably amicably between them. Alternatively, the court could order access to take place at particular times and intervals. One spoke of 'visiting access', or 'staying access'. The latter meant overnight stays.

When parents had not managed to agree their arrangements they would have to issue proceedings and put the matter to the court for a decision about the children.

The Children Act did away with the routine court appointment and the judge making an order in every case. It became a paper process. Parents must now instead file a 'Statement of Arrangements' with the divorce petition. This is supposed to be agreed in advance between the parents and sets out in very brief terms whether anything about the children's future support, living arrangements and 'contact' (not 'access') has been agreed. It is a statement of intent and is not a binding contract. If parents are in agreement, the court makes *no order* about the children on Decree Nisi, other than to express its satisfaction with the arrangements. Both parents continue to have Parental Responsibility. If arrangements for where the child will live ('residence') or how the child will see the non-resident parent ('contact') cannot be agreed, then either parent may apply to the court for an order.

The changes in procedure made a great difference to the way children were dealt with in divorces, and like much of the Children Act was intended to bring about a change in mind set as well. The procedural changes were reinforced by the changes in legal concepts. 'Contact' is not the same as the old concept of access. Access may have been seen as the parent's right to the child. The very term suggests that the child is property to which one is awarded a 'right of way'. Contact, by contrast, has firmly been described judicially as the *child's* right to have contact with his or her parent. Contact can include visits and stays as well as contact by telephone, mail and electronic means. The Act, as we have seen, has attempted to steer parents away from seeing their relationship with children in a legalistic, rights-based way. For the most part this has fitted well with the *Zeitgeist* (the spirit of the age), but some parents still tend, when faced with a dispute with the other parent, to regard their child or children as if they were a commodity, or possession, in which they should have a quantifiable share.

This has become apparent in the discussions in the last few years about whether children should have a main residence with one parent, or whether they should live for some part of the week, or alternate weeks with each parent. This is sometimes called 'shared residence' or 'shared care'. There are campaigners who argue that this should be the statutory norm. Although such campaigners are canny enough to couch their arguments in terms of the child's rights to enjoy its parents equally, there is a tendency when it comes to the reality of working out such proposals to treat hours or days of a child's time as equal units that can be parcelled out mathematically. This approach tends to lose sight of the child's feelings or needs in the matter.

The Children Act 1989 is significant for the way in which it changed the legal concepts surrounding parenthood and removed the lingering legal notion of children as property. The welfare checklist made explicit the principles on which courts had been deciding cases. It can be seen as shifting the focus of the case to the child, rather than the 'rights' of his or her parents. This does not, of course, always make it comfortable for the adults.

Discussion points

In what way do parents still treat their children as property?

Are they right to do so?

Do parents tell their children what to do because they have the power to impose their will on them?

Are they right to do so?

Think of the way your parents thought of their relationship with you. How would you describe it?

Do you think that parental responsibility is a better way of describing the relationship?

Chapter 2
How you become a parent

by Imogen Clout

Legal parenthood including the changes created by The Civil Partnership Act 2004 and The Human Fertilisation and Embryology Act 2008

Since the Children Act 1991 there have been a number of other Acts that have built on its foundation and changed aspects of private family law significantly. Two key Acts have recognised new aspects of being parents that may have seemed very remote in 1989: the Civil Partnership Act 2004 and the Human Fertilisation and Embryology Act 2008.

The Civil Partnership Act allows same-sex couples to form a legal partnership that acknowledges their love for and commitment to each other. The legislation stopped short of simply equating a civil partnership with marriage, but in exhaustive detail went through existing legislation to create a broad equality and equivalence between a same-sex partnership and a male-female marriage. Partly because of the Human Rights Act and European legislation, the Act was careful to make sure that it did not create situations where civil partners would be treated differently (in a discriminatory way) from married couples. Adoption law had to change as well, so that same-sex couples (whether civil partners or not) could adopt. Adoption law was changed further so that unmarried couples could adopt a child together.

This meant that the question of parenthood had to be carefully thought through, because a same-sex couple will not have children together in quite the same way as a heterosexual couple. There will be many instances of step-parenthood, where either or both have children from a previous relationship. Sometimes these children will live with the couple, and sometimes there will be contact. There will also be situations where a child is born during the civil partnership. For lesbian couples, there are a number of circumstances in which a child may be conceived; this may be as the result of artificial insemination, or sexual intercourse that may have been undertaken for the purposes of conception. For male, gay couples, having a child together is more complicated. Adoption is one route, surrogacy is another.

The Human Fertilisation and Embryology Act 2008 is designed to deal with the various permutations of parenthood that have become possible with modern medical techniques. It makes a clear distinction between children born as a result of official, regulated clinical procedures and children who have been conceived in what you might term more do-it-yourself methods. If parents, either same-sex or male-female, undergo fertility treatment in a UK licensed clinic, they will be subject to a process which will find out whether this is a joint decision to which they both consent, or that of the birth mother alone. The status of the other parent – the 'father' or the 'second female parent' depends on these consents.

These new ways of being parents have become law rather quietly. They are not widely known about and there has not been much media attention given to them. Some people find them hard to accept as they offend their sense of what a family or a parent is, or should be. There is a section of opinion that feels that such parenthood offends natural or moral laws, and/or that such parents are being selfish or indulging their desires for children without thought of the consequences. In reality people who become parents in these ways will have probably devoted more thought and heart searching to the process than those who conceive naturally (and sometimes carelessly). It will not have been an easy or risk-free choice.

This is how the law about being a parent now works in England and Wales.

What the law says about becoming a parent

Most people who have a baby don't give very much thought to their legal position as parents. It comes a long way down the list of priorities, well below the choice of names, the baby buggy and the little vests, the interrupted sleep and the feeding regime. Like so much law, it is just there, and assumed to be there, and you are only likely to notice it when there is a dispute, when you and your partner fall out. Couples who are not together at the birth of the child, or who have children by other partners and then come together, may be aware sooner of the legal implications. Even then, they may make assumptions about how the law works that are not correct. Most of us live in a cheerful fog of ignorance about the legal frameworks that underpin our social structures. People who are thinking about having a baby using artificial insemination, on the other hand, may find themselves overwhelmed with the technicalities that they have to consider.

There are now two legal aspects to being a parent: the first is whether you are, legally, related to a child, and the second is whether you have 'Parental Responsibility' for a child. **It is possible to have one without the other.** Sometimes this comes about by simple operation of the law and you have no choice about it. In other cases it depends on the active consent of the 'parent'.

Legal parenthood

A child only has two legal parents at one time, who may not necessarily be the same as his or her biological parents. Normally you will be able to look at the birth certificate or adoption certificate to see who your legal parents are. But this won't always be the case. A single mother, for instance, may choose not to name and register the baby's father on the birth certificate. Adoption or a Parental Order[11] ends the blood relationship and substitutes another person or two people as your legal parents.

---

[11] Following a surrogate pregnancy.

As we have said, English law about family relationships derives from property law. This is significant in the legal relationship of parent and child. The key areas where it matters are inheritance, maintenance and adoption. Your legal children are your 'next of kin', after your husband or wife or civil partner. So if you die without a will, they may inherit part of your estate. They may also make claims on your estate if you do not provide for them[12]. A legal parent can also be compelled[13] to maintain his or her child if the parents are not living together. Only a legal parent can consent to a child's adoption, which can be seen, in crude legal terms, as giving away the property that is the child.

Legal parenthood, by itself, implies nothing about the *relationship* of the adult and child. The majority of legal parents will be living with their children and will have Parental Responsibility automatically, as we shall describe below, but many legal parents do not have it, even if they have 'contact' with their child.

A legal parent is also entitled to apply to the court for what the Children Act calls a 'section 8 order' without first seeking leave (permission) of the court to do so. Section 8 orders are orders for contact, or residence, for 'prohibited steps' (preventing someone from doing something with a child, like taking it out of the country) or a 'specific issue' order (to decide something like the child's schooling, or medical treatment).

---

[12] Under the Inheritance (Provision for Family and Dependants) Act 1975.
[13] Under the various Child Support Acts.

Parental Responsibility

Parental Responsibility sounds obvious, but is, as we have described, a technical legal term created by the Children Act 1989. This means it is fairly new to our legal vocabulary. Whereas legal parenthood can be seen in terms of a property relationship, Parental Responsibility is much more about the personal relationship between an adult and a child. Not all legal parents have Parental Responsibility automatically. Conversely people who are not related to a child by blood or law can 'acquire' Parental Responsibility. It can be shared by three people (or more, in theory, though unlikely in practice). You can also, if you have it, authorise someone else to have Parental Responsibility in your place temporarily. This is what you do when you sign a school trip consent form.

You have Parental Responsibility, once you've got it, until the child is 18. It is possible for a court to remove it, but this is very rarely done.[14]

How does the law work in practice?

Table 1, on the next page shows the various sorts of parents and whether they are related in law and/or have parental responsibility.

---

[14] Lawyers, like theologians, don't like to say 'never'.

Birth	Marriage/ Civil partnership	Adoption/ Parental order	Unmarried	Marriage/ Civil partnership	Unmarried	Living with child
Mother	Father/ second female parent	Both parents: male-female or same-sex	Agreed father/ second female parent	Step-parent	Step-parent	Carer
Related by blood or law AND have Parental Responsibility automatically			Related by law	Not related by law as parents	
				Able to acquire Parental Responsibility. The darker the box, the easier it is		

Let us see how the two concepts, related parenthood, and Parental Responsibility, apply in practice. It is important to note that all parents or all people with Parental Responsibility for a child rank equally. Although a mother gets both legal parenthood and Parental Responsibility automatically at birth, this does not give her better or stronger rights than the child's father.

Mothers
Birth mothers are automatically related to their children by blood and in law. They automatically, from the moment of birth, have Parental Responsibility. Their legal status as the child's parent is severed if the child is later adopted. Adoption also removes Parental Responsibility.

Married male/female couple
The law behaves as though the married male/female couple is the norm of parenthood. When a married couple have a naturally-conceived baby they are both, automatically, the child's related parents and they both have Parental Responsibility. If they later divorce, both these relationships continue.

Any baby born to the wife during the marriage is assumed, legally, to be her husband's child. This is what lawyers call 'a rebuttable presumption'. That is, it may be proved not to be the case. Medical evidence (generally DNA testing nowadays) can establish that paternity is not the husband's. A court can issue a declaration of paternity which enables the details on the birth certificate to be corrected.

If the baby is born to a married woman as a result of fertility treatment in a licensed clinic[15] the husband will not necessarily be the biological father. He may be unwilling or unable to provide the sperm for conception. But, if he has properly consented[16] to the treatment, he is treated in law as though he is the child's natural father[17]. This is likely to be the situation in most cases where a couple are trying to have a baby and it is a mutual decision, but it is possible that a married woman could seek fertility treatment without telling her husband. They might, for instance, be separated, but not divorced.

If the child is given up for adoption, both these relationships end, and the adoptive parent(s) become the child's legally related parent(s), and take over Parental Responsibility.

Civil partners
The law about Civil Partners, as we have described, tries as far as possible to give Civil Partners the same legal position as married male/female couples. Obviously a male or female couple cannot both be a child's biological parents, so the law can't apply in quite the same way.[18]

---

[15] A clinic licensed by the Human Fertilisation and Embryology Authority.
[16] There are formal consent procedures that the clinic will administer.
[17] In the unlikely event that he did not consent he would be treated legally as if he were the child's step-father – see later in chapter.
[18] The rules about fertility treatment changed for children conceived after 6th April 2009.This chapter describes the present law.

Lesbian civil partners

A lesbian couple who are civil partners may have a child using a licensed fertility clinic, where one of them bears the child. The other can become the child's 'second female parent' if she gives the appropriate legal consent to the treatment. She is then, in law, treated as the child's other natural parent from the moment the child is born. The child will legally have no father. Both parents will have Parental Responsibility. These rules also apply if the baby is conceived by some other form of artificial insemination, whether at home, or outside the UK, provided the other female parent agreed to the treatment.[19]

If the other parent did not agree to the treatment at the time, she can only become the child's related parent by adopting the child jointly with the birth mother. This too will extinguish the biological father's connection with the child. Adoption carries Parental Responsibility with it. Alternatively she can agree with her partner that she will simply share Parental Responsibility. This requires less formality than adoption but still has to be effected by making a formal agreement in a prescribed form which is signed, witnessed and lodged at the court. In practical day-to-day matters she will be the child's parent, but they will not be related for inheritance law or the Child Support legislation.

---

[19] If the baby was conceived as a result of sexual intercourse the natural father is the child's related father. The second parent therefore is treated like a step-parent.. See page 37.

Gay civil partners
A gay couple have a different route to parenthood. If they want to have a child together, they can apply to adopt a child together. The Adoption Order will make them a child's legal parents and give them both Parental Responsibility.

Civil partners can also commission a surrogate pregnancy, where a woman conceives and bears a child for them using sperm provided by one or other of them. There are strict rules about the way in which this arrangement is made, and a woman cannot be paid for this service, other than to have her reasonable expenses paid by the couple. Once the child is born *and* if the mother has given the baby to the couple – voluntarily - they can apply for a Parental Order, which, like an adoption order, transfers legal parenthood to the couple.[20] Both parents will then have Parental Responsibility.

If a civil partnership is dissolved
If civil partners divorce this does not change their legal position towards their children; if they have Parental Responsibility this continues.

Unmarried couples
Male/female
The law about unmarried parents is the same whether they are living together or not.

When an unmarried male/female couple have a naturally conceived child both parents are legally related to the child. There used to be a legal

---

[20] This route to parenthood can also be used by a male/female couple.

difference to a child if it was 'legitimate' or 'illegitimate', but this has been abolished[21].

Only the mother has automatic Parental Responsibility for the child. The father can acquire it in a number of ways. For most children the father will be registered on their birth certificates; since December 2003 this will give him Parental Responsibility too. This is the mother's decision, however. The father can't compel her to put his name on the certificate.

If the father isn't registered on the birth certificate, then the mother and he can, later, make a Parental Responsibility Agreement, by filling in the correct court form, signing it at court and filing it with the court.

If the parents marry each other after the baby is born, this too gives the father Parental Responsibility.

If the mother will not agree to share Parental Responsibility the father can apply to the court for an order giving it to him. Courts generally take the view that it is a good idea for both legal parents to share Parental Responsibility but would be reluctant to order it if they felt that the father was likely to use it to be unduly controlling, or where he had, in fact, had almost no relationship with the child.

If the woman has a child by licensed fertility treatment and her partner (who is not the

---

[21] By the Legitimacy Act 1976. The idea still lingers in many people's minds however.

biological father) consents formally to the treatment and to being treated as the father then he will legally be the child's father. He can acquire Parental Responsibility like any other unmarried father: by registering as the child's father on the birth certificate, by Parental Responsibility Agreement, by later marriage, by court order.

An unmarried cohabiting couple can adopt a child together[22] and then they will both be its legal parents and have Parental Responsibility together.

Unmarried couples – lesbian
A lesbian couple who are not civil partners may decide to have a baby using a fertility clinic. The mother's partner can be the 'second female parent' (see page 32). But as they are not civil partners, the second female parent is treated like the unmarried father. She will only get Parental Responsibility if she is registered on the birth certificate, or later enters into a civil partnership with the mother, or they make a Parental Responsibility Agreement together. She, too, if the mother will not agree, can apply to the court for an order[23].

If one of a lesbian couple who are not civil partners conceives a baby without using a fertility clinic, or using a clinic outside the UK, or by sexual intercourse, her partner will not be legally related to the child, unless they subsequently jointly adopt him or her. If the baby was conceived

---
[22] Since 30th December 2005
[23] Section 4ZA of the Children Act 1989 (as amended by the Human Fertilisation and Embryology Act 2008.

by sexual intercourse, or by a private sperm donation, then the child's biological father is legally its father. He is therefore related to the child, and is treated in law as any unmarried father. Adoption by the mother and her lesbian partner would be the only way of extinguishing this relationship.

The partner can also share Parental Responsibility if she can apply to the court for a joint 'Residence Order'. This brings Parental Responsibility with it. If the couple enter into a Civil Partnership then they can make a subsequent Parental Responsibility agreement.
A lesbian couple may also adopt an unrelated child and thus become the child's legal parents.

Unmarried couples – gay
An unmarried gay couple can adopt a child. This would make them both legally related to the child and give them both Parental Responsibility.

Or, they could use a surrogacy arrangement in the same way as a civil partnered couple and apply to the court for a Parental Order.

A single parent
A woman may make a deliberate choice to be a parent by herself.

If the child has a father, whether from a sexual act or sperm donated other than by a licensed fertility clinic, that father is the child's legally related parent and can seek to acquire Parental Responsibility in the same way as any unmarried father. There will be situations where the true father is never told of the child's relationship with him, and the mother does not reveal the father's identity on the birth certificate, and so effectively the child has no father.

There may legally be no father. This would be the case if the child was conceived as a result of licensed fertility treatment without an 'agreed father'.

However, a single woman who is undergoing licensed fertility treatment can ask a man if he will consent to be treated as the father. If he fulfils the 'agreed fatherhood conditions'[24], and consents formally to this relationship, he will be the child's legally related parent and will be able to acquire Parental Responsibility.

Single people of either gender can adopt. In which case he or she would become the child's only related parent.

Step and other relationships

So far we have looked at children born or adopted into a relationship. There are many families where the couple already have children by other partners. Married and civil partner couples are treated differently from cohabiting couples.

In a marriage or civil partnership, step-children will not, of course, be their step-parents' legal children, but the step-parent can be given Parental Responsibility for them. This can be done by a Parental Responsibility Agreement. The step-parent, his or her spouse or civil partner, and the

---

[24] s.37 Human Fertilisation and Embryology Act.

other parent (if he or she is still alive) must all agree to this. This means that Parental Responsibility is now shared by three people. The option of a Parental Responsibility Agreement is not, however, available to an unmarried couple.

Step-parents (married or not) can also get Parental Responsibility if a court makes an order for them to have joint residence or by adopting the child. If both the child's birth parents are alive adoption is unlikely to be ordered by a court, and a court would only make an order for joint residence if it were in the best interests of the child.

If a marriage or civil partnership ends, a step-parent can be made liable to support step-children if he or she has been supporting them during the marriage/civil partnership. If he or she has treated step-children as 'children of the family', the children have a claim for continued support. The courts retain their rights to make orders for step-children, though they can no longer make orders for maintenance of children who are related by blood or adoption because such children are covered by the Child Support legislation.

Unmarried step-parents have no legal financial obligations to their stepchildren.

Other people looking after children.
The law allows other people who are taking a parental role for a child to apply to the court for Parental Responsibility.

Guardians, who are appointed by the court, or have their appointment by the wills of deceased parents confirmed by the court, get Parental Responsibility along with their appointment.

Other people who have been looking after a child for at least three years can also apply for a residence order which would bring Parental Responsibility with it. Sometimes grandparents will use this if they have had the care of their grandchildren. Foster parents can also apply for such an order if the local authority consents and they are either related to the child or have had the child in their care for at least three years.

Summary
If you have read this far in the chapter, you may be feeling completely over-whelmed with the technicality of it all. So on the next page you will find a summary of the different types of parents. We hope it shows how many different, legitimate ways, there are of being parents.

Discussion points

Have there been people in your life who have had a parental role towards you who were not your biological parents?

How would you describe their relationship with you?

Have you had a parental role towards someone who wasn't your biological child?

How would you describe your relationship with him/her?

Do church members fulfil parental roles towards each other?

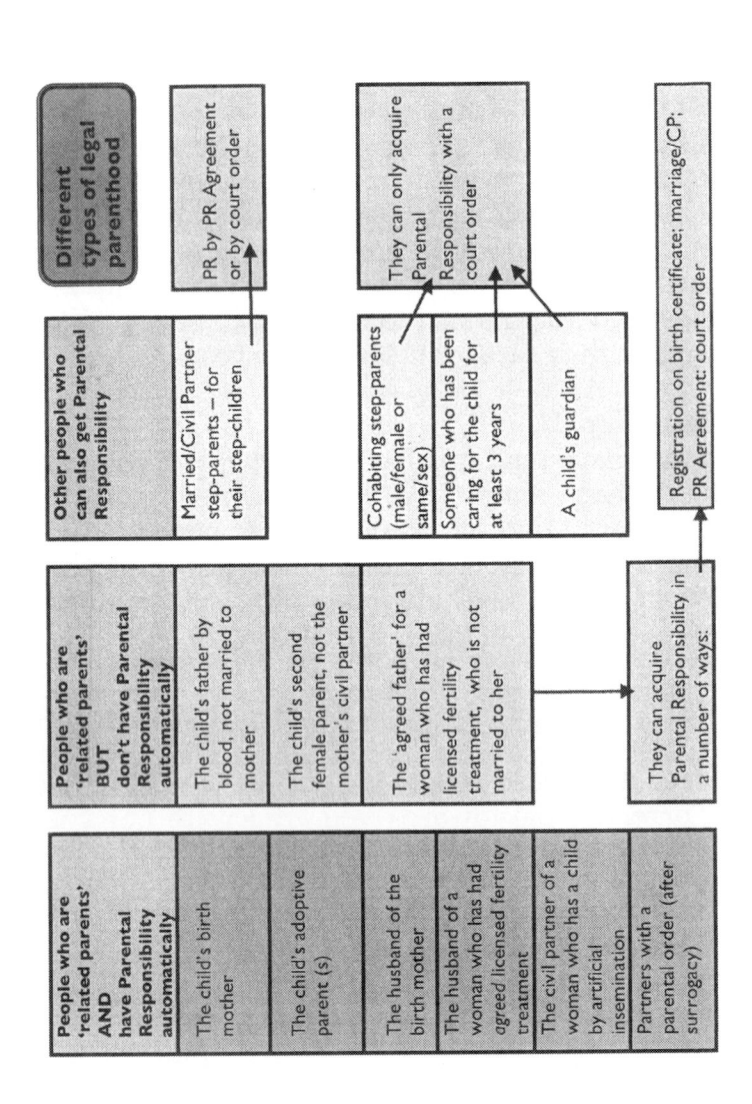

Different types of legal parenthood

People who are 'related parents' AND have Parental Responsibility automatically	People who are 'related parents' BUT don't have Parental Responsibility automatically	Other people who can also get Parental Responsibility	
The child's birth mother	The child's father by blood, not married to mother	Married/Civil Partner step-parents – for their step-children	PR by PR Agreement or by court order
The child's adoptive parent(s)	The child's second female parent, not the mother's civil partner	Cohabiting step-parents (male/female or same/sex)	They can only acquire Parental Responsibility with a court order
The husband of the birth mother	The 'agreed father' for a woman who has had licensed fertility treatment, who is not married to her	Someone who has been caring for the child for at least 3 years	
The husband of a woman who has had agreed licensed fertility treatment		A child's guardian	
The civil partner of a woman who has a child by artificial insemination	They can acquire Parental Responsibility in a number of ways:	Registration on birth certificate; marriage/CP; PR Agreement; court order	
Partners with a parental order (after surrogacy)			

Chapter 3
The legal position of couples

by Imogen Clout

The legal implications of marriage, civil marriage, cohabitation and civil partnership

---

Although civil partnerships have been part of English family law since December 2005[25], there is still some confusion about the terminology and the general legal position, so this chapter is intended to clarify the legal position on couples' relationships.

Marriage
As the law stands at the moment, a marriage can only be legally contracted between a man and a woman. A marriage may be celebrated in a religious ceremony, or a civil ceremony. In either case, in order to be legal, the couple will have had to observe the various technical rules about what notice must be given and requirements about nationality and status. Marriages in the Church of England or the Church in Wales are not subject to the same rules as other marriages.

A civil ceremony is very specifically non-religious: it is not allowed to have any religious

---

[25] The Civil Partnership Act 2004 came into force on 5th December 2005.

content at all. Couples may choose readings and music of their own, provided there are no religious references in them.

There is no distinction in law between a religious and civil marriage: if it is correctly performed the couple are married and their legal obligations to each other are different from those of an unmarried couple.

Most of the law that relates to the rights and duties of a married couple really only comes into focus if the marriage breaks down. The legal state of being married is mostly enshrined in 'common law', that is, it is not set out in statute but relies on legal tradition and precedent, as expounded in legal judgments. One of the aspects of the married life is called by lawyers 'consortium'. This means the entitlement that each spouse has to the company, services and companionship of the other. This includes their sexual relationship. Marriage at one time legalised a sexual relationship: fornication – sex outside marriage – and adultery were at one time punishable under criminal law, as well as being sins, (as traditionally they still are) from a Church point of view.

If the marriage breaks down and the couple divorce, the court has wide powers to rearrange property ownership between them. All their respective assets are potentially divisible or reassignable by the court in its discretion, working within a set of well-established guidelines set out in the Matrimonial Causes Act 1973.

The court can order either husband or wife to transfer property to the other, pay lump sums or maintenance to the other. It also has powers to make provision for children.

On the death of a husband or wife, the remaining spouse will have automatic inheritance rights if there is no will, and tax exemptions will apply to any inherited property.

Civil partnerships
Civil partnerships are in nearly all respects the same, in legal terms, as marriages. At present they can only be contracted in a civil, non-religious ceremony. Like civil marriages, there is a prohibition on any religious content at all. [26]

A civil partnership confers the same rights and duties and legal obligations as a marriage if the relationship breaks down. The Civil Partnership Act 2004 is silent about the nature of the relationship while the partnership subsists. It does not mention the concept of consortium. However, using a combination of equal rights and human rights law, as well as the Act, which says that both desertion, and unreasonable behaviour[27]

---

[26] Since 5th December 2011 a civil partnership ceremony may take place in a religious building, though there is still a prohibition on religious content.

[27] Civil partners cannot use adultery as a 'fact'. This is because adultery has a very specific legal meaning of full heterosexual penetrative intercourse. There are reams of case law about what does and what doesn't constitute adultery. It was easier for the legislators to leave it out as a 'fact' than try to redefine sexual infidelity so that there was a similar definition that would cover both same-sex and male-female

are 'facts' on which a partner may rely to prove that the partnership has broken down irretrievably[28], it would seem that 'consortium' is implied between civil partners. However, and this is possibly significant, whereas a marriage can be declared void if it is not consummated – that is, if the spouses do not have full sexual intercourse – this does not apply to a civil partnership. The Act is silent about the sexual expectations of the relationship.

Many same-sex couples who have contracted a partnership speak of themselves as 'married', and they are expressing the reality of their legal position when they do so. From a practical legal point of view they are as much married as a male-female couple who have contracted a civil marriage.

If a civil partnership breaks down, the legal procedure is called 'dissolution' rather than divorce, but follows the same procedural steps as a divorce, and the court has identical powers in making financial orders for both partners and any children of the relationship.

From a legal point of view it is nonsense for a male-female couple to call for the right to contract a civil partnership, as some have done. Civil partnership is civil marriage in all but name. If what the male-female couple are objecting to is the patriarchal overtones of marriage, and the

---

couples. For a civil partnership sexual infidelity comes within the scope of unreasonable behaviour.
[28] Section 44 (5).

'luggage' of the terms 'husband' and 'wife' then it is up to them to choose the terms that they use.

Cohabiting couples
It cannot be repeated too often that there is no such thing in English law as 'common law marriage'. The law about the position of a cohabiting couple is tough but clear, and applies just as much to male-female couples as same sex couples. Cohabitation does not create any legal relationship or obligation between a couple. When they split up neither can be compelled by the court to pay each other maintenance. The court can only rearrange property ownership between them on the principles of land law, which pays scant attention to their emotional relationship, treating them as though they were partners in a commercial transaction. They have no automatic rights of inheritance from a partner if he or she dies without a will.

Terminology and reality
In September 2011 the Home Office announced that a public consultation on how to make civil marriage available to same-sex couples would begin in March 2012. This provoked a number of expected reactions, including a response from the Church of England that was widely reported as though it was doctrine, rather than a response to the consultation. The consultation has been followed by the confirmation that legislation will be placed before Parliament in 2013.

There is much jealous guarding of the word marriage. But this really comes down to arguing over the word rather than the fact. Same-sex couples can now legally form a quasi-marriage legal bond in a civil partnership. So the argument seems to boil down to whether we change the legal term 'civil partnership' to 'marriage' and amend the legislation accordingly, and/or, allow same-sex couples to contract a 'marriage' in a religious ceremony in the same way as a male-female couple.

If it is simply a question of the name we give to the legal relationship, the simplest option would be to allow same-sex couples the option of referring to their relationship, on official documents, as a marriage *or* a civil partnership, and also to describe their partner as a husband, wife or spouse instead of a civil partner. A same-sex couple could make the choice for themselves, depending on how they wished to be described. This could also be reflected in the wording of the promises made during the civil partnership ceremony.

Some male-female couples have tried to claim that they should have the right to contract a civil partnership. The real distinction, that a marriage is consummated by sexual intercourse, and civil partnership is not, does not seem to have featured in the reported objections of these couples. From a legal point of view their objections do not make much sense. Civil partnership is civil marriage in all but name. If what the male-female couple are objecting to is the patriarchal overtones of marriage, and the 'luggage' of the terms 'husband' and 'wife' then it is up to them to choose the terms that they use. It might be sensible for the wording of a civil marriage vow to be flexible to reflect this too.

We know a number of same-sex couples who describe themselves as married. We also know a number of married male-female couples who refer to their spouses as 'my partner' to avoid what they see as patriarchal overtones of 'husband' and 'wife'.

Perhaps we need to invent a new term entirely, to convey the sense of a lifetime commitment in love and companionship, without the baggage of the patriarchal relationship, but which sounds less businesslike than partnership. The Anglo-Saxon word 'wedd', from which we derive 'wedding', means a pledge, the security given to back up a promise. Perhaps we could call this new institution a 'life-pledge', and the object of our affections our 'life's-pledge'.

Marriage and tradition

Those who want to restrict the use of the word 'marriage', and insist that the traditional meaning of the word should not be diluted or encroached on, should think about what the word really does mean. It is inaccurate to suggest, as Cardinal O'Brien has recently, that the teaching of the Church about marriage has been consistent for the past 2000 years[29]. The attitude of the Church to

---

[29] The Cardinal's comparison with slavery was, from his point of view, an own goal. He suggested that redefining marriage would be like making slavery legal. The implication of his remark was that slavery was obviously an evil to which the Church would be opposed. In fact, the abolitionists of slavery faced great opposition from the Church, which taught that it was supported as an institution, by a number of references in the Bible. Christians who opposed slavery had to find new ways of looking at

marriage has shifted over the centuries. Marriage was originally regarded as a poor second to the celibate life. The early Church, as we describe (in Chapter 5) followed the teaching of Paul (1 Corinthians, 7, vv 8-10) that it was best to remain single, but if you could not exercise self control it was better to marry than burn with lust. Marriage really only became an approved state of being after the Protestant reformation[30].

Anglican critics of legalising 'gay marriage', refer to Canon Law, often saying that it defines marriage as the union of a man and a woman. In fact Canon B30 says:

> *'...marriage is in its nature a union permanent and lifelong, for better for worse, till death them do part, <u>of one man with one woman</u>[31], to the exclusion of all others on either side, for the procreation and nurture of children, for the hallowing and right direction of the natural instincts and affections, and for the mutual society, help and comfort which the one ought to have of the other, both in prosperity and adversity.'*

The words 'one man and one woman' suggest that what the framers of the Canon had in mind was not the possibility of a same-sex union, which would not have occurred to them at that time, but to emphasise that marriage was monogamous, as opposed to the polygamy found in the Old Testament, or in Islamic law. The traditional

---

scriptural authority and argument to counter these 'Bible-based' justifications.

[30] Erasmus wrote *'In Praise of Marriage'* 1519, which was widely influential

[31] our emphasis

teaching of the Church has not been about the possibility or otherwise of a same-sex marriage because this, historically, has not been a social reality.

A marriage now is not at all the same institution that it was in biblical times, or even a century ago. In the past marriage has been a patriarchal institution where the husband has had powers of life and death and ownership of the wife and any children of the relationship. Marriage ceremonies were effectively property transactions, where the chattel woman was handed over from her father to her husband. We still have a trace of this in the custom of the bride being brought down the aisle by her father and 'given away'.

If we say that marriage is somehow hallowed as a relationship that can only exist between a man and a woman, we should be aware that the traditional sense of this is a relationship which legally sanctions an unequal power balance. On the whole, the Church has preserved and approved that patriarchal relationship. When St Paul describes the Church as Christ's bride, (Ephesians 5: 22-33) he means to convey that the Church is subservient to and possessed by Christ, as well as being loved. The wife's marriage vow, has, until recent times, contained the promise to obey her husband.

To be sure, there is Christian teaching which runs counter to this. Paul's injunction to husbands to love their wives (Ephesians 5:25) may seem commonplace to us, but was radical in its time: love was not the normal foundation of the marriage bond. Christ's prohibition against divorce, (Mark 10: 1-12) which may now sound illiberal and oppressive, radically protects the woman who can otherwise be discarded by her husband as a piece of unwanted property.

Marriage as a relationship in which two *equal* partners, because of their love for each other, pledge publicly to share their lives together in a way that does not give one of them power over the other, is a truly modern idea, and it is still not the reality for many married couples. The incidence of domestic violence and abuse – it is estimated that one in four women has suffered this - indicates that there are many relationships in which the power balance is still skewed in favour of men, at least in their view.

We suspect that what really bothers people about the use of the word 'marriage' for same-sex couples is the implication that 'marriage' makes sex between the couple licit. So if same sex couples are 'allowed' to call their relationship a marriage, by implication their sexual relationship is not one that can be forbidden.

'Marriage', at the moment, does have a specific legal meaning which restricts it to a legal relationship between a man and a woman. But the word is also used widely as a metaphor for a meeting of two things or people that are compatible and complementary. One might describe parma ham and melon as being a marriage of flavours. The partnerships of Galton and Simpson, the script-writers, or Morecambe and Wise, the comedians, might be described as 'marriages made in heaven'. No-one, encountering these metaphorical uses of the word, would ask, which is the male and which the female? Instead, we accept the ideal use of the word to convey the way in which the two elements go together perfectly, and make a whole.

If we took the legal view of the word, given all its historical baggage, one might wonder whether any same-sex couple would truly want to describe their relationship as a marriage. But the metaphorical use of the word should explain why it is a very real issue. Love and mutuality demand a term less cold than civil partnership. Somehow, it sounds as a second best alternative to marriage, even if this is not the legal reality. Also, as we have seen, marriage implies consortium and a sanctioned sexual relationship. And thus it is tied up with the question of a religious ceremony for same sex couples. Because this is really what the debate is about.

Conclusion
Recent legislation has increased the possible number of types of family. Prior to this legislation the following possible types of family were those of children living with their natural parents, or living with a divorced parent, or living with a divorced parent who had remarried, or living with a single, unmarried, parent. Also, adoption, guardianship or fostering could create a family unit. Even prior to recent legislation, then, the idea that a family consisted essentially of a married (heterosexual) couple and their natural children did not correspond to the facts. The recent legislation has made the situation even more complex. In our opinion, the present debate on whether or not gay and lesbian couples should

be allowed to marry focuses upon the wrong issue. It focuses upon the legal relationships between men and women whereas it should be concerned with the quality of family life and the mutual bonds between children and those who have Parental Responsibility for them within the law.

Discussion points

We will all have very different ideas about marriage, springing partly from our beliefs and partly from our experience.

For a group discussion:

Ask each person to write a short (no more than say 25 words) definition of marriage. Then discuss what they have written with a neighbour. Ask them, if they can, to identify what they have drawn on in coming up with their definition: is it their life experience, the teaching of the church or the Bible, their knowledge of the law?

Pool the suggestions of the group on a flip-chart and see whether you can reach a broad consensus – or do you need to differ and put down a number of different view-points?

Chapter 4
What does the Bible say?

by J W Rogerson

A consideration of Biblical teaching and examples of family life and parenting

---

The Bible is the principal text to which Christians turn for guidance in human relationships. For some Christians, indeed, it is the only text that they would regard as valid. We therefore need to consider how the text is to be considered and used. There is a widespread ignorance of the content of the Bible, even among regular churchgoers, and any responsible use of the Bible requires that its content should be known before the problem is addressed of how that content can or might be used.

One way of using the Bible when considering what guidance it might give to Christians in the matter of family relationships is to privilege certain texts and to ignore the remainder of what the Bible said. In support of this approach it can be argued that this is precisely what the early church did, a subject to which it will be necessary to return. Let us therefore explore the family structures that we encounter in the Old Testament

Using the Bible – Old Testament precedents
Genesis 2:24 'therefore a man leaves his father and his mother and cleaves to his wife, and they become one flesh' has been appealed to as a creation ordinance that lays down the principle of 'one man, one woman, for life'.[32] This kind of approach can be strengthened by appeal to Mark 10.6-9 where Jesus refers to Genesis 2.24 in a debate about whether it is lawful for a man to divorce his wife. If this line is followed, any form of human liaison that differs from one man, one woman is deemed to be contrary to the will of God as expressed in a creation ordinance and endorsed by the teaching of Jesus. Why would anyone want to disagree with such apparently overwhelming authority?

The main reason would be that if, in fact, Genesis 2.24 does mean 'one man, one woman' many people portrayed in the Old Testament were either unaware of this, or if they were aware, deliberately ignored the creation ordinance. No one is censured in the Old Testament for having more than one wife, or for entering into surrogacy agreements. In one instance, Levirate marriage, a form of surrogacy, is actually commanded, as will be shown below.

---

[32] See M. Green, 'Homosexuality and the Christian' in M. Green, D.Holloway, D.Watson, *The Church and Homosexuality. A Positive Answer to the Current Debate*, London: Hodder and Stoughton, 1980, p.27.

The fact that Old Testament families were, or could be, polygamous (i.e. that a man could simultaneously have two or more wives) is shown by the following examples. Jacob married the two sisters, Leah and Rachel (Genesis 29.15-30). This arrangement, known as sororate marriage (from Latin *soror* meaning sister), and explicitly prohibited in Leviticus 18.9, is well known in social anthropology.[33] Jacob's brother Esau had three wives, Judith, Basemoth and Mahalath (Genesis 26.34, 28.9). Moses had two wives, the Midianitess Zipporah (Exodus 2.21) and an unnamed Cushite (i.e. Ethiopian or Sudanese) woman (Numbers 12.1), although it has been argued that Zipporah and the Cushite woman were the same person, or that Zipporah had died before Moses married the Cushite woman.[34] Gideon is described as having seventy sons and many wives (Judges 8.30) and although we are not told how many wives had been taken by some of the so-called minor judges, the number of their sons implies that they had more than one wife. Jair (Judges 10.4) had thirty sons, Ibzan (Judges 10.4) had thirty sons and thirty daughters, and Abdon (Judges 12.14) had forty sons and thirty grandsons. The father of Samuel, Elkanah, had two wives, Hannah and Peninnah (1 Samuel 1.2), David had seven (1 Chronicles 3.1-9) and Solomon, infamously, had seven hundred wives

---

[33] See A Committee of the Royal Anthropological Institute of Great Britain and Ireland, *Notes and Queries in Anthropology*, London: Routledge and Kegan Paul Ltd., 6th ed. 1954, p. 118.
[34] See Matthew Poole, *A Commentary on the Holy Bible* (1685), Edinburgh: The Banner of Truth Trust, 1962, vol. 1, pp. 285-6.

and three hundred concubines (1 Kings 11.3)[35] Ahab is credited with seventy sons (2 Kings 10.1). These many indications of polygamy occur in narratives that also imply monogamous states of affairs. For example, there is no indication that Noah had more than one wife, nor that his sons did (Genesis 7.7). Again, Genesis 24 is a long narrative about Abraham's search for a suitable wife for Isaac. The chosen bride, Rebekah, seems to remain Isaac's only wife. Lot seems to have had one wife (Genesis 19.15). Perhaps these narratives reflect the fact that for many of the presumed hearers/readers of those traditions, there was no possibility of their having more than one wife. Polygamy was most likely a privilege of the wealthy and mighty in society. The many sons provided by polygamous arrangements could be married off and strategically appointed to offices in such a way as to enhance the power and influence that the family could exert. This certainly seems to be the implication of notices such as that in Judges 10.3-4, where Jair's thirty sons are said to have ruled thirty cities. It is also important to note that the legislation in Deuteronomy 21.15-17 specifically provides that where a man has two wives, the son of the older wife will inherit the major share of his estate. Again, the laws against incest in Leviticus 18.7-18 indicate a polygamous situation because the person addressed (Ego) is forbidden to have sexual relations with his father's wife as well as

---

[35] The Hebrew word *pilegesh,* traditionally translated as 'concubine' is of disputed meaning. It denotes a status below that of 'full' or 'regular' wife, but in what way is not clear. David is said to have had ten concubines (2 Samuel 20.3), whose job it was to 'care for the house' when David fled from Jerusalem because of Absolom's revolt.

with his own mother, that is to say, it is assumed that the father of the person addressed (Ego) will have wives in addition to the woman who is Ego's mother.

The Old Testament portrays polygamy as a fact of life, whether or not 'ordinary' people were able to take advantage of it. Another fact of life appears to have been surrogacy in at least two forms. The first, in order of narrative priority in the Old Testament, is what might be called informal surrogacy, although it implies a clear legal understanding that a man's female slave is his property, as are children that she may bear. It is found in the stories of Abraham and Jacob. Because Sarai (Sarah) is barren, Abram (Abraham) has sexual relations with his wife's Egyptian maid, Hagar, as a result of which a son, Ishmael, is born (Genesis 16.1-4). Jacob's second, and favourite, wife Rachel, is also barren and, desirous of children, gives her maid, Bilhah to Jacob so that she may have children credited to her (Genesis 30:1-8). It is noteworthy that when sons are born to Bilhah, Rachel describes them as her own offspring. She names the first son Dan, saying, 'God has judged me, and has also heard my voice and given me a son' (Genesis 30.8).[36] When the second son is born Rachel says 'With mighty wrestlings I have wrestled with my sister, and have prevailed' (Genesis 30.8). Not to be outdone, Rachel's elder sister, Leah, having passed the age for child-bearing, gives her maid, Zilpah, to Jacob, who produces two sons for her (Genesis 30.9-11). These stories of informal surrogacy presumably made sense to their intended hearers/readers; that

---

[36] The Hebrew name Dan means 'he judged'.

is to say, the hearers/readers were familiar with informal surrogacy arrangements, and would not have found the stories surprising or scandalous. They indicate that this form of surrogacy had not only implications for the provision of an heir who would inherit property, but were a way of rescuing barren women from the social disadvantages of childlessness.

Legislated, as opposed to informal, surrogacy is found in Deuteronomy 25.5-10. If a man dies childless and has brothers, it is the duty of the (elder) brother of the deceased to have sexual relations with the widow in order to have a son who will perpetuate the name of the deceased, and inherit his property. This form of marriage is called levirate marriage, from the Latin *levir* meaning brother-in-law, and is practised in a number of societies.[37] According to the passage in Deuteronomy 25, if the brother refuses to act the widow can arraign him before the elders who sit in judgement in the city gate. If the brother persists in his refusal, the widow can publicly pull off one of his sandals, and spit in his face, and the man's reputation will be tainted with this disgrace.

There are two narratives that have levirate marriage as an important factor in their plot structure. In Genesis 38, the daughter-in-law of Judah, Tamar, becomes a childless widow, and her brother-in-law refuses to have intercourse with

---

[37] *Notes and Queries in Anthropology*, p.117; R. G. Abrahams, 'Some Aspects of Levirate' in J. Goody (ed.), *The Character of Kinship*, Cambridge: Cambridge University Press, 1973, pp. 163-174.

her. God punishes him by bringing about his death. Tamar then plays a trick on her father-in-law, and causes him to father twin boys by her. A more edifying story is that of the Moabitess Ruth, in the book of Ruth. She is a childless widow who has returned to Bethlehem with her mother-in-law Naomi. A kinsman of Naomi, Boaz, then marries Ruth. This is not strictly levirate marriage because Boaz is not Ruth's brother-in-law. There is a man who is a closer relative to Naomi than Boaz (we are not told exactly how the man and Boaz are related to Naomi) and he refuses to marry Ruth. In this case it is Boaz who arraigns the man before the court of elders, and the man who takes off his own sandal. The details of the narrative do not match the law specified in Deuteronomy 25.5-10, but there are similarities. What is important is that the son that Ruth bears to Boaz is said to be Naomi's. 'A son has been born to Naomi' proclaim the women (Ruth 4.17). Ruth and Boaz have been surrogates for Naomi. Naomi now has a male heir who can inherit her husband's property and thus provide for her.

Whether or not adoption was practised in ancient Israel has provoked much discussion among experts, with some denying that there was any such thing.[38] In English translations of the Bible the word 'adopted' in the sense of someone taking parental responsibility for a child who is not a natural son or daughter occurs at Esther 2.7 and 15, describing the relationship between Mordechai and his niece Esther. The Hebrew says

---

[38] See H. J. Boecker, 'Anmerkungen zur Adoption im Alten Testament', *Zeitschrift für die alttestamentliche Wissenschaft* 86 (1974), pp. 86-89.

that Mordechai had 'taken her to (be) (a) daughter'. In Exodus 2.10 it is said in respect of Moses and the daughter of Pharaoh that 'he became her son'. Other passages that have been taken to indicate adoption include Ruth 4.16, where Naomi 'took' the child who had been born to Boaz and Ruth, and Genesis 48.5 where Jacob says to Joseph that the sons Ephraim and Manasseh who had been born to Joseph in Egypt 'are mine'. A much-discussed passage is Genesis 15.2-3 where it has been argued that Abram had adopted a slave to be his heir because his wife was childless. While it may be accepted that some of these alleged proofs for adoption are questionable, there seems to be no doubt that passages such as Psalm 2.7 'you are my son, today I have begotten you' imply that the Israelite king was believed to be adopted into a special relationship with God on his coronation,[39] and it would be strange, if this were so, if there were no corresponding social arrangement or convention of adoption.[40] Adoption may not have been common in ancient Israelite society but it is going too far to say that it did not exist at all.

New Testament teachings
So far, the discussion has centred on the Old Testament, apart from the reference to Mark 10.6-9. What of the New Testament? The first thing to point out, even if it seems offensive at first sight, is that the birth of Jesus was a surrogate birth. According to the Infancy Narratives of Matthew

---

[39] Boecker, ,Anmerkungen', p. 88.
[40] See the discussion by F.W. Knobloch, ,Adoption' in *Anchor Bible Dictionary* vol. 1, pp.76-79.

and Luke, Mary did not have sexual relations with Joseph. Indeed, Matthew 1.18-25 relates that when Joseph discovered that Mary was pregnant he resolved to divorce her. In Old Testament law (Deuteronomy 22.23-28) intercourse with a betrothed virgin was a capital offence punishable by the stoning to death of the woman and the man who had slept with her. Later Jewish interpretation of the passage found ways of softening the harshness of the sentence, and by New Testament times adultery had become a ground for divorce.[41] The passage in Matthew reflects this situation and explains what, to Matthew's Jewish Christian readers/hearers, would be the problem caused by a betrothed woman being found to be pregnant. Matthew 1.25, which says that Joseph 'knew her [Mary] not until she had borne a son' has been taken in much Christian exegesis to mean that Mary and Joseph never had sexual relationships, and that Mary remained a virgin all her life. Although it is highly unlikely that this is what the verse means, it is a reminder that, paradoxically, the Holy Family, so much presented as the ideal for family life was, according to traditional Christian belief, a family in which mother and father abstained from sexual relationships.

Another interesting passage is 1 Timothy 3.2, which specifies that a bishop must be 'the husband of one wife.' This can be interpreted in two ways: that it was in order for church members

---

[41] H. L. Strack, P. Billerbeck, *Kommentar zum Neuen Testament aus Talmud und Midrasch*, vol. 1, Munich: C.H.Beck, 1926, pp.51-2; Mishnah Tractate *Gittin* IX, 10 where the school of Shammai interpreted Deuteronomy 24.1 in terms of unchastity.

in general to have more than one wife, except for bishops (i.e. overseers) who were restricted to one; or, that a bishop who became a widower was not allowed to remarry. The second interpretation would imply that church members were to be monogamous. Whatever is meant exactly, Strack-Billerbeck provide evidence that, even if rarely, polygamy persisted in Judaism well into the early Christian centuries.[42]

Biblical family structures
The Latin word *familia*, from which the English word 'family' comes, denoted a household, in which everyone in the household, whether related or not, came under the absolute authority of the male head of the house. The Hebrew equivalent, *bet 'āv*, means literally 'father's house', and functioned in the same way. The sabbath law (Exodus 20.10, Deuteronomy 5.14) prohibits work on the sabbath to non-related members of a household as well to as related members. Those mentioned are servants and sojourners (i.e. people estranged from their own kin who enjoy the hospitality and protection of the household). Cattle (in Deuteronomy 5.14 'ox or ass or any cattle') are also included. The sabbath law gives a snapshot of a typical (probably well-to-do) family. A similar, if larger, picture is provided at Deuteronomy 16.11, where the celebration of the feast of weeks is to include the Levite (possibly here a priest from a redundant sanctuary who is dependent upon a household), the fatherless and widows. This larger picture indicates a household that has wide-ranging obligations to people who would otherwise be excluded from economic and

---

[42] Strack, Billerbeck, *Kommentar*, vol.3 pp.647-650).

social support. On the other hand, the head of a household had the power to sell his children into slavery (Exodus 21.7, Nehemiah 5.5), or expose a daughter (i.e. abandon her to die, Ezekiel 16.4). The law in Deuteronomy 21.18-21 about the treatment of a stubborn and rebellious son may indicate an attempt on the part of the legislators to restrict the power of a father to kill his son because of persistent disobedience. The boy's parents are required to bring the boy before the elders in the city gate and to gain their approval before the boy can be stoned. The fact that heads of households had this power did not mean that they exercised it. While Abraham is portrayed as willing to sacrifice his son Isaac (Genesis 22.1-10), David is reluctant to take action against his son Amnon. When the latter rapes his half-sister, Tamar, and when Tamar's full brother Absalom has Amnon killed, David only punishes Absalom by exiling him (2 Samuel 13).

     The Hebrew *bet 'àv* was a unit within a larger descent group called a *mishpachah*, a word that is sometimes translated as 'clan', although it is questionable whether it is accurate to use terms such as 'clan' and 'tribe' in relation to the Old Testament.[43] This larger unit was important for the purposes of defence, and was possibly the group from which was drawn the *go'el,* the kinsman whose duty it was to avenge anyone who was murdered by a member of a different descent group (Numbers 35.25). It is interesting that when Saul is introduced in the narrative at 1 Samuel 9.1, he is identified as the son of Kish, son of Abiel, son

---

[43] See J.W. Rogerson, *Anthropology and the Old Testament*, Oxford: Blackwell, 1978 pp. 86-101.

of Zerar, son of Bechorah, son of Aphiah, i.e. in terms of his great-great-great-grandfather. This helped to identify him in relation to other groups and individuals who shared common descent from the more remote ancestors in the lineage.

The help afforded by the wider family group could be enlarged in cases where the whole people was thought of as a kin group, so that the word 'brother' could mean 'fellow Israelite'. This is found in the Deuteronomic legislation, for example, in Deuteronomy 15.2-3, 7-11, 12-18, where Israelites are commanded to remit debts every seven years, and to release from slavery any Israelite who has been forced into that situation. In these passages the Hebrew word *'ách*, normally translated as 'brother', means 'fellow Israelite'.[44] A further step is taken in Leviticus 25, where an attempt is made to abolish slavery completely, by commanding that any brother (i.e. Israelite) who reaches the point where he cannot maintain himself economically, is to be taken into the family household and given the status of a sojourner (Leviticus 25.35-41). Indeed, the passage implies that the brother Israelite will not enter the household alone, but will come with his own household (Leviticus 25.41). A narrative example of a household welcoming someone in need is found in 2 Samuel 9.1-8, where David gives refuge to the surviving son of Jonathan and perhaps adopts him.

Turning to the New Testament, the early church was established in a Graeco-Roman world

---

[44] E. Otto, *Theologische Ethik des Alten Tesatments*, Stuttgart: Kohlhammer Verlag, 1994, pp. 186-192.

in which the family was a household that included slaves, lodgers and adopted children.[45] There was no one Greek word that denoted this institution, the nearest equivalent being *oikia*, closely related to *oikos* meaning 'house'. Where the word 'family' occurs in English translations of the New Testament, and it occurs rarely, it is not usually a rendering of *oikia*. For example, when the Philippian gaoler is baptised together with his family, the Greek means literally 'all those of his' (*hoi autou pantes*). Again, in Mark 3.21, when the family of Jesus comes to take charge of him, the Greek rendered as 'family' is literally 'those from beside him' (*hoi par' autou*).

The passage in Mark 3 portrays Jesus as having a radical view of the family. In verses 33-5, when told that his mother and brothers are looking for him, Jesus replies that his mother, brother, and sister are those who do the will of God. In Luke 8.1-3 those who accompanied Jesus on his preaching journeys are said to include several named women. This could be seen as a kind of alternative family united around a leader and a common mission. In the early chapters of the Acts of the Apostles the Christian community is said to practise community of goods (Acts 4.32-6). On his arrival in Corinth, Paul stays with Aquila and Priscilla (Acts 18.1-3), and in Caesarea with Philip the evangelist (Acts 21.8). It is evident that on some of his travels, Paul was accompanied by a number of fellow-workers (Acts 20.4-5). John

---

[45] See C.Harrison, 'The Silent Majority: the Family in Patristic Thought' in S. C. Barton (ed.), *The Family in Theological Perspective*, Edinburgh: T & T. Clark, 1996, pp.88-91.

19.26 describes how Jesus, whilst on the cross, commanded the disciple whom he loved to take his mother Mary into his household. What these passages seem to indicate is a new idea of the family, a family based not upon the possession of property or on blood relationships, but on a shared commitment to the service of the Gospel.

Crucial to any account of the family in the New Testament are the so-called Household Codes. These are found in Colossians 3.15 – 4.1, Ephesians 5.22 – 6.9 and 1 Peter 2.18 – 3.7, and deal with relationships between husbands and wives, fathers and children and masters and slaves. To this extent they reflect the household nature of the family, presided over by the male head. Slightly more fragmentary, and less comprehensive 'codes' are found in 1 Timothy 2.8-15 and 6.1-2 and Titus 2.1-10 as well as early Christian texts such as the Didache, the letter of Barnabas, the first letter of Clement and the letters of Ignatius and Polycarp.[46] It has long been recognised that these 'codes;' are not peculiar to the New Testament and can be paralleled from contemporary Graeco-Roman society, although they are distinctively Christian where they give loyalty to God and Christ as the reason for obedience and mutual love (e.g. Colossians 3.22-4). Dunn describes them as instances of 'household management'[47] and outlines some of the views that have been expressed about their significance. An important point is that the earliest churches took the form of house churches,

---

[46] See the useful charts in J.D.G.Dunn, 'The Household Rules in the New Testament' in Barton, *Family*, pp.44-46.
[47] Dunn, 'Household Rules', p.49.

whose members could be drawn from Jews and Gentiles, slaves and free men, and men and women. These assemblies were unusual in the context of their society, and rules were needed to ensure their orderly functioning. This is why the 'codes' appear in the context of reference to Christian worship (e.g. Ephesians 51.19-20, Colossians 4.16-17) and some of them refer to positions in the church (1 Timothy 3.1-12). 1 Timothy has a section on widows, their responsibilities and their relation to the church. In other words, the 'Household Codes' are attempts to describe what good 'household management' should be like in the special circumstances of the life and mission of Christian communities in the late first century A.D. and the second century. These attempts took the best practices of the surrounding societies and adapted them to Christian purposes, although in some cases they seem to have broken with the accepted class conventions of the time. When Pliny was sent by the emperor Trajan to reorganise the affairs of the province of Bithynia in AD 112 and investigated the local Christians, he got information by torturing two deaconesses, who also happened to be slaves.[48] It is interesting that these churches appear to have disregarded Old Testament laws, such as the obligation to release slaves at the end of six years of service (Exodus21.1-6, Deuteronomy 15.12-18). It is, in fact, remarkable how little attention the early church paid to Old Testament legislation.[49]

---

[48] J. Stevenson, *A New Eusebius. Documents illustrative of the history of the church to AD 337*, London: SPCK, 1957, p.14.
[49] For a discussion of the neglect of the Old Testament and its gradual rehabilitation as a source of moral and social

What does the Bible say about parenting?
A brief consideration of this question will conclude this chapter. The subject of parenting in ancient Israel reveals two sides of the matter, the formal and the personal. Formally, the male head of house had absolute power over his children. Children could be exposed (i.e. left to die immediately after birth – Ezekiel 16.4-5) or sold into slavery (Nehemiah 5.5). If a son was stubborn and rebellious he could be brought before local elders and be stoned to death (Deuteronomy 21.18-21). On the personal side the power of human affections created strong bonds of love and care. The mother of Samuel, Hannah, who had dedicated her son to God's service at the sanctuary of Shiloh, made and presented him with a robe on her annual visit to Shiloh (1 Samuel 2.19). Rebekah greatly favoured her son Jacob at the expense of his twin brother Esau, and was willing to connive at his deceit in tricking Esau out of his father's blessing (Genesis 27.1-40). David's love for his son Absalom was such that he took only the mildest action when Absalom had his brother Amnon killed (2 Samuel 13.37-9) and was distraught at Absalom's death, even though it occurred in the course of Absalom's armed rebellion against his father. David's lament is one of the most poignant in the Bible:

> O my son Absalom, my son, my son, Absalom! Would I had died instead of you, O Absalom, my son, my son! (2 Samuel 18.33, Hebrew 19.1)

---

guidance in the church see J.W. Rogerson, *According to the Scriptures? The Challenge of Using the Bible in Social, Moral and Political Questions*, London: Equinox 2007.

Parenting analogies applied to God imply the personal rather than the formal side of the matter. 'As a father pities his children, so the LORD pities those who fear him' exclaims the psalmist (Psalm 103.13). The unknown prophet of Isaiah 40-55 allows that a woman might forget her sucking child, but reassures the people of Israel that this cannot be so with God. In Psalm 22.9 the psalmist likens God to the midwife who took him from his mother's womb and laid him upon her breasts. The early chapters of the book of Proverbs are cast in the form of a father instructing his son in the ways of wisdom (Proverbs 2.1 – 7.21). In the moving story told to David in 2 Samuel 12.1-5, the ewe-lamb belonging to a poor man is described as having been like the man's daughter. 'It grew up with him and with his children; it used to eat of his morsel, and drink from his cup, and lie in his bosom'. It is important to mention these aspects of parenting because it is all too easy to think only of passages from the Book of Proverbs such as that in Proverbs 13.24: 'He who spares the rod hates his son, but he who loves him is diligent to discipline him', and to represent 'biblical teaching' as enjoining the stern and physical disciplining of children. While we would not deny the value of caring for children within the context of clearly defined boundaries, with appropriate sanctions if they are crossed, the whole approach should, in our view, be tempered by respect for children, and their own integrity.

The importance of the personal aspect of parenting in the Bible is that it is a reminder that laws and formal conventions do not exhaust the range of human relationships and behaviour. Too often in the history of the church the Bible has been used as a law book, concerned with regulating the formal and legal aspects of human relationships. Yet, as Paul observed when describing the fruits of the Spirit – love, joy, peace etc – against such there is no law (Galatians 5.23) and the same is true of those manifestations of human affection that spring from the deepest parts of human nature. Yet these things are hardly taken into account when the Bible is looked to for guidance to order human relationships. Law overwhelms grace and mercy.

Discussion Exercise

This can be used as an introduction to a discussion of scriptural authority and precedent. You can use it with a large group, assigning small groups a family each to consider, or as a quiz. The characteristics can be copied, cut into strips, and people can be asked to pin them onto a card for the correct family.

Suggested answers and scriptural references can be found on page 183.

Can you match the Old Testament families to the characteristics in the following list?

Abraham's family

Jacob's family

Moses' family

David's family

Surrogacy arrangement
Long marriage
Child sacrifice
Childlessness
Second marriage
Step-brothers
Concubines
Marriage breakdown
Polygamy
Love match
Childlessness
Surrogacy arrangement
Sibling rivalry
Concubines
Death in childbirth
Sex with sister-in-law
Sex with daughter-in-law
Passionate same-sex relationship
Polygamy
Adultery
Grieving over baby death
Family rebellion

Concubines
Adopts lover's child
Foreign marriage
Child mutilation
Adoption
Sibling rivalry
Death in childbirth

Chapter 5

Families, the law and the Church

By Imogen Clout

We examine the historical structures of families, the legal framework and the way that the Church has treated them

---

A story from my husband's family
In 1817 the Poor Law authorities transferred a young widow, Catherine Lake, with her two children, Thomas, aged 2 years and 8 months, and Mary, aged 8 months, from the parish of Stoke Damerel to the parish of Wembury, Devon. Seven years later the parish apprenticed Thomas to his uncle by marriage, Martin Wills, in Saint Mellion, Cornwall.
Thomas married in 1841. His bride was his employer's daughter. She was 16 and pregnant when they married. By 1851 they had three living children – their eldest drowned aged 4 - and Thomas was working as a miller. By 1861 they had eight living children and history repeated itself. Thomas's household had been joined by a servant/apprentice George Body, who, the next year, married his eldest daughter Mary. He was 19 and she was 17 and pregnant when they married. Their first baby died three months later; they went on to have fifteen more children, five of whom died in infancy. Their youngest surviving child, Ivor, never met his two eldest brothers, who had settled in Australia and America before he was born.
Ivor is my husband's grandfather.

Families have always been complex and untidy structures. Anyone who has tried to trace their own genealogy and has had the investigative pleasure of seeing their ancestors' census records from the nineteenth century, will have found 'jumbled' households, with step-parents, half brothers and sisters, cousins and grandchildren living *en famille,* children born before marriages, children born out of wedlock. There are families who have taken in other children and brought them up as their own. There are households with servants and apprentices. On a normal family tree diagram it is often hard to convey the complexity of relationships.

Against this, English law, based traditionally on property, might be thought to have had an elegant (if brutal, to our modern sensibilities) simplicity. Before the twentieth century the primary purpose of family law was to regulate property rights. The only legal ties that the law recognised were those of blood within legally recognised marriage. Wives and children had limited status, being more akin to property than persons; feelings and human emotions were scarcely relevant legal factors.

There are three broad influences on the regulation by church or state over family structures: economic and property considerations; morality and its sister, respectability; and human feelings of love, desire and sentiment. The third has, for the last two thousand years, been much less significant. The law was heavily influenced, historically, by property and financial considerations, and, to a slightly lesser degree, by morality. In England and Wales, historically, most family law matters were not dealt with by the common law but by the Church courts. Church regulation has tended to be principally influenced by moral codes, which set out what is held to be right or wrong in behaviour. Such morality derives for the most part from Scripture, as set out in the Old Testament, and from teaching in the New Testament. This might suggest to us that the approach of the Church comes from a higher authority and is in some way superior to the secular law. We need, however, to be aware that much of the family law that is found in Scripture has, as its basis, considerations of 'purity' or 'property'.[50]

As far as both Church and state are concerned feelings of love and desire are to be regulated and tamed; human passions need to be kept firmly under control. This is made quite clear in the preamble to the Solemnization of Holy Matrimony in the 1662 Book of Common Prayer:

…it is not by any to be enterprized, nor taken in hand, unadvisedly, lightly, or wantonly, to satisfy men's carnal lusts and appetites, like brute beasts that have no understanding; but reverently, discreetly, advisedly, soberly, and in the fear of God; duly considering the causes for which Matrimony was ordained.
First, It was ordained for the procreation of children, to be brought up in the fear and nurture of the Lord, and to the praise of his holy Name.
Secondly, It was ordained as a remedy against sin, and to avoid fornication; that such persons as have not the

---

[50] See L. William Countryman, *Dirt, Sex and Greed*, London: SCM Press, 2001 (new ed.)

gift of continency might marry, and keep themselves undefiled members of Christ's body.
Thirdly, It was ordained for the mutual society, help, and comfort, that one ought to have of the other; both in prosperity and adversity.[51]

Note the order of the reasons why marriage is ordained: first for children, secondly for the regulation of lust, with the suggestion that marriage is a poor second best to celibacy, and only thirdly for mutual support. As far as the Book of Common Prayer is concerned, marriage is a way of making human relationships tidy and controlled. And note further, the absence of the word 'love' anywhere in the reasons for marriage. This is tough language, the impact of which is perhaps obscured by its age and elegant cadences. It is completely at odds with a modern sensibility which would say that the reason for getting married was because a couple loved each other and wanted to have a sexual relationship, and wished to acknowledge and confirm that relationship publicly.

False nostalgia
Nevertheless we tend to cling to an idea that in the past – a vague notion that we are careful not to define – the family was a better structure, and more ordered: that people lived lives that were voluntarily more regulated and, dare we say, respectable, and this was much more desirable. 'Family values' have become a modern political cliché, especially claimed by the right wing as a good thing. Everything, it seems, would be better

---

[51] The Alternative Service Book (1980) did depart from this, with much more emphasis on love.

if people married and did not cohabit, and those marriages lasted for life, if there were no single parents, and no – oh horror! – 'broken homes'. On the 'Today' programme on 28th April 2011 Gavin Poole from the Centre for Social Justice think tank, claimed that the problems of child poverty could be addressed by strengthening families, implying that the increase in cohabitation was a root cause of the problem. His opponent, Polly Toynbee, asked how the government was going to change this. They couldn't, she pointed out, *make* people get married. Wouldn't it be better to support the reality of modern family life?

The slogan 'family values', or sometimes, 'Victorian values' carries with it the idea that there was once a time when everything was better. There is a heady false nostalgia for this land of lost content. Television reinforces this. The popularity of such programmes as 'Lark Rise to Candleford' and 'Downton Abbey', encourages us to think about the past as a time when people may have been poor, but they were happy, where family structures were strong and respectable and everyone knew their place, where deference from the poor and lowly was rewarded by a sense of *noblesse oblige* from the benevolent upper classes. However, a close reading of Flora Thompson's memoir on which 'Lark Rise' was loosely based, shows that life was far harder and less rosy than the television portrayal. We are too easily seduced by our longings for a simpler, happier time.

We seem to have a collective nostalgia for a period we vaguely remember, located somewhere in the 1950s and early 1960s. It is a sanitised fictional world, characterised by the families in the school 'reading books' and Ladybird books from that era. In those pictures little girls are in skirts, boys in shorts – often wearing ties, fathers wear braces and smoke pipes and the pretty mothers wear hats and gloves outside the house and spotless aprons in the kitchen. Home is a neat and tidy haven. Even the pets are cute. These images from this period are very powerful; they, too, exercise a nostalgic charm.

David Kynaston, who with good reason entitles his social history of 1951 – 1957 'Family Britain', says:....*'one can plausibly argue that in some sense British society was 'frozen' during the ten or so years after the war, that there was for most people, following the shake-up of the war, an instinctive retreat to familiar ways, familiar rituals, familiar relations, all in the context of only very slowly lifting austerity and uncomfortably limited material resources.'* A harking back to these times is not completely irrational. For many people they were good times, made all the sweeter by the contrast with wartime conditions.

Middle-aged and older people may well recall their childhoods as rosy times of greater certainty and stability. People had fewer material possessions, and took greater care of those they had. Family sizes had tended to drop as birth control became more widely used. Health, particularly maternal and infant health, improved under the new National Health Service. Fewer mothers worked and children came home from school at mid-day for their dinners. Mothers sewed home-made clothes and knew how to mend and knit. Fathers knew how to do carpentry and fix their cars, if they had them. Food was simpler, and home-prepared. Fish and chips was an occasional treat. Labour-saving devices such as vacuum cleaners, washing machines and fridges were becoming more common, but married women with families were still discouraged from working. As a result many mothers had much more time to spend with their children and husbands in domestic and leisure activities. Holidays were spent in this country: you learned to swim in freezing British waters and appreciate sand in your sandwiches, and crisps that had little blue screws of salt that you had to shake into the bag and only came in two other flavours[52]. If there was a child in your class whose parents were divorced it was only whispered about. It was very important to be respectable; you didn't eat in the streets, you wore a hat to church, and boys took their caps off indoors. ITV, when it came, was thought to be a good deal less respectable than the BBC. 'Common' was a disapproving adjective, and people did not hesitate to use it where they felt that it applied.

But we seem to have got stuck in a time warp. Somehow, this idea about family life, in the teeth of the reality, has become the popular idea of what a Christian family is, both inside and outside the church.

What is a 'Christian family?'
Our churches are not immune to this. Churchgoers subscribe to the cliché of the Christian family just as much as politicians. We can see this if we consider what the cliché of a 'Christian' family

---

[52] Cheese and onion, and salt and vinegar, introduced in the late 50s/early 60s

looks like? We do not mean by this the 'Church family', which is a different concept. We are thinking of the family unit that the phrase 'Christian family' might evoke for churchgoers, or that people who are not practising Christians might imagine if the phrase were to be used.

A Google image search for "Christian family" is revealing. There are plenty of smiling family groups, often posed closely together. They look happy and tidy, and most of them are immensely clean and shiny – cleanliness is obviously next to godliness in this context. Although there are some large family groups, there is a prevalence of the two parents and two children (one boy and one girl) image, especially in logos and cartoons. Images that have been created for clipart, which parishes and churches may use in their published material and on their websites, mostly show families like this. One local church we know has a similar family painted on its notice board – presumably to show how welcoming it is.

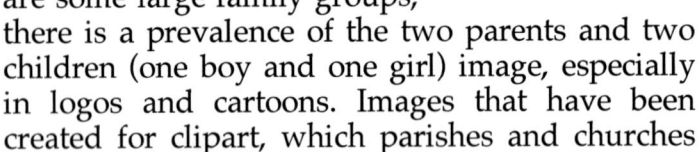

It's easier to see how people outside the church might form a view about what they think Christians think. It is perhaps more puzzling why people who feel that they are Christians should cling to this notion when they are well aware that their own families bear little relation to the cliché. Is it another example of false nostalgia for an imaginary period when we all looked as though we were in a Ladybird book? Or is it a stubborn clinging to an ideal? Just as we know we should be kind, forgiving and forbearing, but are conscious that we slip from this regularly, do we somehow feel that our family life *should* take this peaceful old-fashioned form?

Historical perspective

Let us instead consider what the reality of family life is and has been for almost all of the past two thousand years. The structures of family life known to early Christians were governed by Jewish and Graeco-Roman law and custom. There are some differences between Jewish and Roman law, but for both, the family unit defines who and what you are in society: your legal status. The family and the household (*familia* in Latin) are interchangeable concepts, including not only the immediate family but all other related dependants, domestic servants and household slaves. (*Famulus(a)* is the word for a household slave.) The male head of household, the senior father, was the person who had power including powers of life and death over all the other members of the household. Only he could own property, and that included the other household members. He could sell a child into slavery if he chose. In Roman law a woman remained under her father's control (*potestas*) even if she was married. She was not in law related to her husband's family.

Within a family, or household, there was a clear hierarchy of rank, power and obedience. Men came highest up the rankings, women and minor children below that, and household slaves below that. This order was seen as part of the natural structure of things, of the cosmos. The family was a microcosm of the state. Family members owed obedience to the head of the family, just as he owed obedience to the emperor, or head of state, just as humans owed obedience to God. To disobey, or injure your parents was more serious than just an expression of a personal dislike; it was a threat to the natural order akin to treason or blasphemy.

It would be a mistake to think that because of this legal structure families were not places where husbands loved their wives and parents loved their children. We know that love has always been a human emotion and a tender foundation of many marriages and households. Both Plato and Aristotle recognised that the bonds of affection and friendship between husband and wife and the love that both would have for their children were key to the healthy family unit. *Patria potestas* does not turn all men into abusive despots; it goes hand in hand with notions of duty and honour, of mercy and respect. But it is affection that functions in a household in which the cultural and legal assumption is that there are fundamental and unalterable inequalities between men and women.

From a modern standpoint we might feel that this somewhat diminishes the idea of love, although if we take this stance, we are being wilfully blind to the fact that even if we think of ourselves as living in an enlightened age, the majority of men will regard themselves as superior to the women in their households, both intellectually and financially.

Against this background Jesus' and Paul's teaching about the family can be seen as subversive of an institution in which people are chattels under the power of one man, rather than a framework of love and grace. The last verses of Matthew Chapter 22, where Jesus is told by the crowd that his mother and brothers are outside wanting to speak to him, are often quoted as suggesting that Jesus was 'anti-family'. This is an over-simplification, and does not fit with what the Gospels tell us, elsewhere, of Mary's devoted following of her son, or his brothers' actions after his death. It is consistent, however, to read this passage as Jesus' challenging reaction to the popular assumption that your kin-folk had a prior claim on you because of the power structures of the family and the duty that that implied. Instead of that, he says that the people to whom you owe duty and allegiance are those bound to you by love and companionship. To our modern ears, Paul's instruction to husbands to love their wives might sound rather trite and obvious; to his contemporaries it was a statement that the foundation of the family as an affectionate relationship, not a property transaction. Jesus' teaching on divorce, which condemns the ability of a man to get rid of his wife as if he were discarding an object, again recognises that a wife should be treated as a person in her own right. The practices of the early Christians, sharing their goods, eating together as though they were all equal in rank, recognising the role of women in leadership, undermine the power and hierarchy of families in their traditional sense.

In the first few centuries of its existence the Church was not altogether approving of the idea of marriage. Celibacy was the ideal, but pragmatism recognised that this was not everyone's calling. Marriage was certainly better than fornication. As we have seen from the Book of Common Prayer, you weren't supposed to be marrying so that you could enjoy sex together, and this had been the official attitude of the Church for centuries. Once you were married, however, the teaching of the Church about divorce was much stricter than the Jewish or Roman law and custom that preceded it[53]. It is often pointed out that the Church's teaching on divorce would not have been so difficult to live with in the past because people 'then' did not, or would not expect their marriages to last for decades. But that modern gloss suggests that couples were making actuarial bets on each other's lifespan when they made their vows. It also takes a modern view of divorce which suggests that divorce is to be viewed as a potentially good, liberating thing.

Divorce cannot acquire this aspect except in a society where women have equal legal status with men and can achieve a level of financial independence. Without these safeguards divorce

---

[53] Because of Jesus' teaching on divorce (Matthew 19. 3-12, Mark 10. 2-12)

will always be an aspect of power that men can use to control and discard their wives. A woman who is aware that her wage-earning power is severely limited, and her status as a divorced woman will shut her out from much of society, (and has no social benefits scheme that she can turn to) is not going to think that divorce will bring her happiness.

Before the modern period marriages tended to be shorter in length, because of shorter life expectancy; marriages were broken by death rather than divorce. As life expectancy grew in the 18th and 19th centuries, so did the lengths of marriages. Even so, a large proportion of children were brought up by widowed mothers, a smaller proportion by widowed fathers. This was also the case after the two World Wars. Politicians who incline to blame many of society's ills on single-parent families would do well to remember this. Widows and widowers did, of course, remarry. In the mid-nineteenth century about 15 percent of men and 9 per cent of women who married were recorded as being widowed. This meant that in many families there were complex step and half relationships.

In contrast to what we might believe about the respectability of our forefathers and mothers many children were born or conceived out of wedlock. In 1859-60, a period when, we might presume, Victorian values made people more sexually continent, 6.5% of births in England and Wales were recorded as illegitimate; in Scotland the rate was 9.1%. Earlier in the century the rate is estimated at about 20%. In 1939 the Registrar General of Births Marriages and Deaths engaged in the mathematics more commonly entered into round the village pump and estimated that about 30% of all first children born in the previous year had been conceived before their parents' marriages.[54] The figures for mothers under 20 suggested that at least 42% were pregnant when they married. The percentages continued to be high in the decades that followed. In the early nineteenth century the figures had been higher still, with 'an estimated 20% of illegitimate births and over half all first births being conceived outside marriage'[55].

In the early modern period (1500 – 1800) the penalties for pre-marital intercourse could be severe, particularly if sex resulted in pregnancy and the birth of a bastard child. An unmarried mother could be sent to a house of correction, and publicly flogged. Fathers could also be punished, especially if they attempted to evade their financial responsibilities towards a child. It was a serious matter for the authorities, not so much, one suspects from a puritan disapproval of the pleasures of fornication, as the financial burden that such a relationship might impose on the system of parish relief. At the same time there seems to have been an understanding that a couple who intended to marry, whether informally or after a betrothal, might have sexual relations, on the clear assumption that if a

---

[54] Statistical Review of England and Wales for the Years 1938 and 1939
[55] 'Happy Families' by Professor Pat Thane. Pub. British Academy Policy Centre: www.britac.ac.uk/policy/Happy-families.cfm

pregnancy resulted, a marriage would follow[56]. This arrangement seems to have been so common that, if it was not quite respectable, it was scarcely scandalous. The marriage would make the child legitimate and ensure that the man had a financial responsibility for the mother as well as the child. In some cases, because of this legal responsibility, parish authorities did what they could to compel a marriage. Parson Woodforde records in 1768[57] marrying a man brought to the church in handcuffs in case he ran away.

Many people did not marry at all – about one in ten in the population over the 18th and 19th centuries, with the figures being higher for women than men, generally because there are more women than men in the population. This may have been chiefly for economic reasons; people had to be able to afford to set up their own homes before they could marry, or face unrelieved poverty. The figures, though, should not be taken to imply that all unmarried people lived celibate lives by themselves. Many couples could not marry because of previous marriages that they were unable to dissolve because of the legal and financial difficulties. We can therefore safely assume that many couples lived together 'in sin', but would have done so discreetly so as to avoid social ostracism. They would therefore have presented the appearance of a married couple to the outside world. The poor had less incentive to

---

[56] This had the practical advantage that the woman's ability to conceive was proved, an important consideration if one of the purposes of marriage is to secure an heir.
[57] Entry for 22nd November 1768

marriage than people for whom the property and inheritance implications of marriage mattered.

Such 'common law'[58] marriages were common enough by the early 20th century to be recognised by legislation. In World War One service men's 'unmarried wives' were recognised, as were their illegitimate children from such relationships (even when they had legal wives). Other legislation also recognised these relationships. They may have had official disapproval as not being 'respectable', but the government was pragmatic enough to realise that there was a large enough number of such relationships to make the legislation necessary.

In earlier times, in the sixteenth and seventeenth centuries, family structures were even less regulated. Marriages might take a number of forms, some according to canon law, some according to folk custom. Couples might live together and be treated in their community as married, without ever having gone through a ceremony recognised by Church or state authorities. The richer your family, the more likely it was that there were formalities, so that property was secured and inheritances regulated. It was only in 1753 with Lord Hardwicke's Marriage Act, that the state finally managed to impose order and rules on the practice of marriage and lay down definitively what English law would accept as a valid marriage[59]. A marriage was to be null and

---

[58] The term is misleading: there is no such legal status in English law as popularly supposed. See Chapter 3.
[59] The Roman Catholic world had regularised the canon law about marriage at the Council of Trent in 1563.

void unless it was recorded in a parish register and signed by the bride and groom, at least two witnesses and the clergyman who officiated at the ceremony. The church had a duty to send a copy of the marriage register to the diocesan bishop each year, so that the records could be preserved. Genealogists have reason to be eternally grateful to Lord Hardwicke.

The impulse for this reforming legislation was the legal chaos that was piling up as a result of what Lawrence Stone[60] calls an 'extraordinary explosion of clandestine marriages between 1660 and 1753'. Moral considerations aside, the real problem with unregulated marriage and the questions of legitimacy and illegitimacy that it throws up, are the legal property considerations. English law of inheritance until the 20th century relied heavily on primogeniture - property passing from father to eldest legitimate son - with only legitimate children inheriting automatically from their fathers. Most families with property would have taken steps to set up trusts and entails to make sure that property passed that way. Women, who in law would lose their property rights to their husbands on marriage, could also have their entitlements protected by trusts set up in anticipation of their marriages. Men had duties to support their wives and children, including their illegitimate children if paternity was acknowledged or proved, otherwise this burden might fall on the parish. Irregular marriages made these legal obligations harder to enforce and gave rise to costly litigation.

---

[60] In Stone, L., 1992 'Road to Divorce: England 1530 -1987' Oxford, OUP 1992

Although the 1753 Marriage Act was successful in stopping the rash of clandestine marriages, it seems to have created a two tier system where the poor tended not to avail themselves of church weddings, though there are other social reasons, as we have seen, why poorer couples might not feel the need for a religious ceremony. Dissenting couples, that is, people who worshipped other than in the Church of England, also resented having to marry in their Anglican parish church. In 1836, in recognition of this, civil ceremonies in register offices, which were cheaper than church weddings, became legal[61]. This did not, however, make them particularly popular. By the beginning of the 20th century, only a fifth of weddings were civil ceremonies. It was only in 1992 that the number of civil ceremonies in England and Wales overtook religious ceremonies. By 2009 civil ceremonies accounted for 67 per cent of all ceremonies. Part of the reason for this recent increase may be the relaxation since 1995 of the law about where marriages might take place. Couples now have a wide choice of secular venues, which many feel much more romantic and appealing than a municipal hall. Marriage numbers have generally declined since 1972. Lawrence Stone suggests that our modern customs of cohabitation and marriage now resemble the situation that prevailed in early modern England.

A modern change in legal sensibility
We have moved in the law from seeing blood (and property) ties as the only, or most significant, family connections, to treating families as

---

[61] Marriage Act 1836, which also allowed Catholic and non-conformist weddings to be legally recognised.

emotional units, bound together by love and care and the responsibility that comes with these feelings, properly exercised. These legal changes have happened rather suddenly (in legal terms, where time tends to the geological scale). The modern view is that family law is about more than just property rights, but this has been, like all things legal, a slow development. Older married women will recall their difficulties in entering into financial agreements for loans or hire purchase without their husbands' consent. As far as the lenders were concerned, the Married Women's Property Acts might as well not have been passed. It was as late as 1991 that the House of Lords settled that a man cannot use the fact that he is married to his wife as a defence if he rapes her[62]. Before that the legal assumption was that marriage had given him proprietary rights over her body. Only in 1998 did the right to respect for family life enter English law in the Human Rights Act, and what does and does not constitute a family under this legislation is a developing legal area. The Human Rights Act also prohibits discrimination on any ground such as (inter alia) sex, marital status, or, by implication, since it does not state this in terms, sexual orientation. Children, it should be noted, are 'humans' too.

In the last twenty-five years, as we have seen in Chapters 1 and 2, the law about parents and children has changed substantially. Legislation now recognises, particularly in the case of children, that feelings and emotional ties need to be taken into account in judicial decisions. The welfare of a child is now seen as involving

---

[62] In the case of R v R [1991] UKHL 12 (23 October 1991)

more than the practical arrangements for where he or she is to be housed, educated and fed; the child's emotional welfare must also be attended to. Judges are regularly asked to consider a child's feelings and wishes and to take into consideration the quality and style of their relationships with their parents. It is possible now for legislation to be proposed to amend the Children Act 1989 so that it requires a court to consider:

> ……………*that children have the benefit of both of their parents having a meaningful involvement in their lives; ………… that children receive adequate and proper parenting to help them achieve their full potential;*
> *…………….. that both parents fulfil their duties, and meet their responsibilities, concerning the care, welfare and development of their children.*[63]

Such language, and such considerations would not have been considered appropriate or even necessary in legislation before the Children Act 1989. The law is, it seems, at last treating the family as an emotional and social unit, recognising as parents people who have these ties with their or other people's children. This, inevitably makes the laws about parenthood much more complicated than they were, but it reflects the nuances and complications of family life.

The Church needs to learn a lesson from this. We should be alert to the changes in the law and realise that many people regard themselves as

---

[63] From the Shared Parenting Bill, a Private Member's Bill presented to Parliament on 13 July 2010. The Government indicated in the Queen's Speech on 10 May 2012 that it proposed to bring in legislation influenced by this.

parents who do not fit tidily into the structures that church liturgies and ceremonies are designed to acknowledge. We should also be concerned that we tend to conflate the outward appearance of the family with its inward structures of grace – love, nurture, and understanding, and assume that you don't have one without the other. Tidiness and cleanliness are not to be confused with godliness.

We are unfortunately seduced by an idea of a Christian family which derives heavily from the idea of the Holy Family, mother, father and well-behaved child. Somewhere in our heads this idea, conveyed by countless old masters, and less distinguished, but nonetheless potent cheap art, has stuck and created for us a paradigm of peaceful nuclear family life, in which a single docile child plays happily in the shavings below the carpenter's bench and learns to lisp his prayers at his mother's knee. A Catholic prayer on the web can say, without a trace of irony:

Grant us, O Lord Jesus,
to imitate faithfully the example of your Holy Family
and to make our home another Nazareth.[64]

Google "Holy Family" images and you will get the same sort of picture. Jesus is often shown with curly blond hair. These are powerful images and paradigms, and we are influenced by them perhaps more than we are aware.

When we asked groups of Christians to respond to images of the Holy Family we got a broadly approving appreciation of 'family values', 'tranquillity', 'love', 'harmony'. When we asked the same groups later to write down words that

---

[64] www.catholic.org/prayers

summarised their own families, or to draw a picture of those families we got a response that was messy, noisy, loving, complicated, imperfect. The fact is that real family life is a long way from these pretty images. It is, in the first place, a good deal less peaceful and tidy. It is often noisy, bad-tempered, rivalrous and chaotic. Divorce, separation, death, illness, disability, cohabitation, all disrupt and restructure our lives. Some families will live as isolated nuclear units, others still live together or close to each other in clusters of many generations. Families can be dangerous and dysfunctional places, capable of inflicting great and lasting damage. They can also be full of life and laughter, caring and support.

Families are places where emotions swing wildly. One moment a sister will be screaming at another that she hates her, she really hates her. Doors will slam, meals will be abandoned, tears will pour. On the next day, or even in the next hour, there will be hugs and cuddles, treats and smiles. Couples will row, and make up. There will be weeping *and* laughter at funerals. A mother who feels taken for granted will suddenly feel better when a sticky, badly spelled card for Mother's Day appears at breakfast. Meal-times, bringing much needed blood sugar levels up, are great restorers of good temper.[65]

Families that work well are capable of holding all these contradictions and changes within them. They are bound together by love, and shared experience, which has transforming

---

[65] Table fellowship takes on new significance when you think about it like this.

power. They are little heavenly kingdoms in which repentance and grace are constantly renewing and rebuilding relationships, and give them strength and energy. Families that work well also have great power to attract people who are not related family members to them and include them in their family life. Hospitality is a great feature of such families. They draw other people in and give them a place.

Instead of clinging to an idea of family life that uses the cliché of the Holy Family as its yardstick of how things should be, we should be looking at real families. For they can teach us that this is the model for the Kingdom of Heaven – not a static place of perfection, peace and calm, but a place where real life flourishes and where love and forgiveness are constantly renewed and refreshed.

Discussion Exercise

Write down on one side of a piece of paper a number of adjectives that you think describe your family and family life. Don't try to censor them, or think very lengthily about it: write what comes to mind.

Then do a Google search for 'holy family' and choose Images. Look at the first ten or so, and on the other side of the paper write adjectives that come to mind when you look at these.

Now compare the ways of describing these families. Where does reality lie?

If you have any knowledge of your family history, consider how 'tidy' it was, and what varieties of family structure it contained.

Chapter 6
Christian family practice

by J W Rogerson

How what the Bible says about families has been used in Christian tradition, and discussed by theologians

---

Early Christian communities
Generally speaking, the pattern of the family established in early Christian communities was that of the Roman household, with the absolute authority of the male head. This pattern, indeed, maintained itself legally until the middle of the 20th century. It could appeal to the 'Household Codes' of the New Testament, and their assertion of male headship (Colossians 4.18, Ephesians 5.22). In the early church, however, this pattern was also challenged in several ways: by what was taken to be the example and teaching of Jesus, by the teaching of Paul, by asceticism, by assertions of independent roles for women, and by the monastic and hermit traditions. These overlapped to some extent. As has been pointed out, Jesus taught (on one occasion) that his mother, brothers and sisters were all those who did the will of God (Mark 3.33-35). He is also reported to have said

that becoming a disciple involved hating father, mother, wife, children and brothers (Luke 14.26, Matthew 10.37). In his own life he was unmarried. He is also reported as saying that discipleship involved selling all of one's earthly possessions (Matthew 19.21).

The teaching of Paul implied that marriage was a second-best arrangement compared with celibacy. 'It is well for a man not to touch a woman' he wrote in 1 Corinthians 7.1, and he continued 'but because of the temptation to immorality, each man should have his own wife and each woman her own husband'. Later in the chapter he advised the unmarried and widows to remain single but conceded that if they lacked self-control they should marry. 'For it is better to marry than be aflame with passion' (1 Corinthians 7.8-9).

Asceticism, that is, the deliberate rejection of material possessions, and the adoption of a life of various kinds of abstinence was not an invention of Christianity, but was to be found in the Jewish and Graeco-Roman worlds from which Christianity emerged.[66] But where asceticism was embraced by Christians, it could be justified by appeal to the teaching of Jesus and his way of life as described in the Gospels, and by the teaching of Paul. In particular, abstinence from sexual relationships with women could be justified on the ground that Jesus did not marry. There was also the expectation in the very early days of

---

[66] See the article by J. Bergman 'Askese I', L. Markert, 'Askese II', J. Maier 'Askese III' and J.Gribomont 'Askese IV' in *Theologische Realenzyklopädie* vol.4, pp.195-225.

Christianity that Jesus would soon return in glory (1 Thessalonians 4.13-5.11) and that there was no point in begetting offspring, not to mention the belief in Greek circles that the 'flesh' and human sexual intercourse were 'unclean'. It also had the effect of liberating women from having to have sexual relations with men. Texts such as the 2nd century AD *Acts of Paul and Thecla* show how a high class young woman could reject marriage and the subservience that went with it, and exercise an important ministry as a Virgin. [67] In one way, this was an extension of what is clear from the letters of Paul: that he valued the ministries of his female fellow-workers (Romans 16.1-16). Further, and against the 'headship' teaching of the 'Household Codes' some married women saw their true head as Jesus or the local bishop.[68]

These tendencies or movements must be seen in the light of the fact that marriage and the family were, and are not, specifically religious institutions. A difference between the Old and the New Testament is that the former arose within a distinctive nation, whereas the latter was produced by a tiny, and often persecuted, religious sect whose members lived in a world where the family and marriage were regulated by

---

[67] See M.R.James, *The Apocryphal New Testament*, Oxford: Clarendon Press, 1924, pp.272-281 for the story of Thecla, who is inspired by Paul's preaching to follow the way of chastity.

[68] A. Rousselle, 'Die Familie im Römischen Reich: Zeichen und Gebärden' in A. Burgière et al (eds.), *Geschichte der Familie* vol 1, Darmstadt: Wissenschaftliche Buchgesellschaft 1996, p.373. French original *Histoire de la famille*, Paris: Armand Colin 1986.

the civic authorities. It is not surprising that the early church ignored the Old Testament when it came to the family, because the distinctively ethnic laws and narratives of the Old Testament had no relevance for Graeco-Roman society. A change came about with the triumph of Christianity in the early part of the 4th century. Even so, it was a very long time before the churches were able to play a major role in the regulation of marriage and family affairs.[69] Where the churches did have power, namely, over their own members, the Bible was used in the following ways.

An important weight was attached to Genesis 2.23-4 as confirmed in the teaching of Jesus in Matthew 19.4-5. Marriage was ordained by God, and was indissoluble. On the basis of Ephesians 5.22-3 which states that a husband is the head of his wife as Christ is the head of the church, it was maintained that marriage was a human symbol of the union of Christ with the church. At the same time, and perhaps to bring under ecclesiastical control young women who wished to emulate role models such as Thecla, virginity was allowed without this diminishing the value of marriage. Texts that were cited (not altogether convincingly for modern readers) were Matthew 22.30 'in the resurrection they neither marry nor are given in marriage' and 1 Corinthians 7.32-34, where Paul outlines the advantages for men and women who do not marry when it comes to 'the affairs of the Lord'. From the 5th century, a concern to avoid incest led

---

[69] L. Brink, 'Ehe/Eherecht/Ehescheidung VI' in *Theologische Realenzyklopädie* vol 9, pp.330-332.

to attention being paid to Leviticus 18.[70] This chapter, together with the Genesis 2.24 principle that men and women through marriage became 'one flesh' determined the kin relationships within which marriage was permitted, although dispensations could be given by the Pope where there were urgent political needs. Henry VIII had married his deceased brother's wife, a liaison prohibited by Leviticus 18.16, by means of a papal dispensation. He could, of course, have claimed that his was a levirate marriage since his bride was a childless widow whom it was the brother-in-law's duty to marry; but levirate marriage was not, apparently, seen as a possibility in Christian practice.

Another passage of the Bible that became important was Matthew 19.21, 29. This states that if one wishes to be perfect, then all goods and possessions must be sold, and then says that there will be a reward in heaven for those who have forsaken house and family and lands for the sake of Jesus. This was one of the key passages justifying the so-called religious life where men and women took vows of chastity, poverty and obedience and lived in monastic communities that had various aims according to the visions of their founders. People who followed this calling embraced, in effect, a radical and alternative way of family life. A monastery was a household, presided over by a male or female head, whose members were bound together by the vows that they had taken. The bridal imagery in some female religious orders, with a ring worn to show

---

[70] H. Cronzel, Ehe/Eherecht/Ehescheidung V' in *Theologische Realenzyklopädie*, vol 9, pp.325-327.

attachment to Christ, indicates the 'family' nature of such institutions, as does the fact that the title Abbot is derived from the Semitic words for 'father', and monks and nuns are called and address each other as 'brother' and 'sister'

The development of a theology of Christian marriage
As time went on after Christianity became the official religion of the Roman Empire, the church increasingly took control of the regulation of marriage and family relationships, with far-reaching, and surprising (to modern readers) results.

According to Bede's *Ecclesiastical History*, Augustine, Archbishop of Canterbury (597-604) sought the advice of Pope Gregory I on various matters, including marriage.[71] Goody has reconstructed from this material the following state of affairs obtaining in England in the 6th century:
- Close marriage (e.g. marriage between cousins)
- The Levirate (and marriage to affines, i.e. 'in-laws')
- The sending out of children to wet-nursing and adoption
- Concubinage [72]

---

[71] Bede, *Historical Works* I, (Loeb Classical Library 246) Cambridge, Mass: Harvard University Press; London: Heinemann, 1962, pp.122-125.
[72] J. Goody, *The Development of the Family and Marriage in Europe,* Cambridge: Cambridge University Press, 1983, p.204

According to Goody, the church took steps to counteract each of these features and to establish a quite different pattern of marriage and family relationships.

It is well known that marriage between cousins is a way of ensuring that property stays in the possession of the narrower kin group.[73] Cousin marriage is not explicitly mentioned in the lists of prohibited liaisons in Leviticus 18 and 20, and although there is no direct reference to cousins marrying in Old Testament narratives, it is related that Isaac married the daughter of his cousin Bethuel and that Jacob married the daughters of his uncle Laban (Genesis 24.15; 29.13-30. The relationships are set out diagrammatically in Rogerson and Davies.)[74] Marriage with a cousin is not prohibited in Britain today.[75] However, in his reply to Augustine, according to Bede, Pope Gregory explicitly banned marriage between cousins on two grounds: that such marriages could produce no children (a proposition contradicted by the practice of cousin marriages in many societies) and that it was forbidden by the holy law (*sacra lex*), presumably that in Leviticus 18.[76]

---

[73] J. Beattie, *Other Cultures: Aims, Methods and Achievements in Social Anthropology,* London : Routledge & Kegan Paul, 1964, p.129.
[74] J. Rogerson, P.Davies, *The Old Testament World,* London: T. and T.Clark International, 2nd ed. 2005., p. 31.
[75] P. Beesley, *Anglican Marriage in England and Wales. A Guide to the Law for Clergy.* London: Faculty Office of the Archbishop of Canterbury 3rd ed. 2010, p.46.
[76] Goody, *Development,* p.50; Bede, *History*, pp.124-5.

Levirate marriage, which Jesus certainly did not condemn (Matthew 22.23-33) was also forbidden by the church from the end of the fourth century[77] while mediaeval canon law extended the prohibition to include affines (people related by law).[78]

Adoption, which had been so important in the Roman Imperial households, was forbidden from the fifth century. It did not feature in United Kingdom law until 1926 although there were, of course, other ways of ensuring that property was inherited by people who were not related to each other, if that was the purpose of adoption in a particular case.[79]

According to Goody concubinage was also condemned by Pope Gregory in his letter to Augustine, although he gives no page reference to Bede, and there does not appear to be any mention of concubinage in Gregory's letter as reported by Bede.[80] If concubinage is understood as the taking of an additional wife in order to provide a legal heir (which is how it operated in the Bible in the case of Abraham and Hagar, Genesis 16.1-6) it seems that this practice gradually came to an end in Christian circles in Norman England.[81] The method adopted was to regard the children born in such secondary marriages as illegitimate and therefore unable to claim the status of heir. As Goody nicely remarks, 'under Christianity, the

---

[77] Goody, *Development*, pp.60-61.
[78] Goody, *Development*, p.56.
[79] Goody, *Development*, pp.100-101. 73.
[80] Goody, *Development*, p. 75.
[81] Goody, *Development*, pp.76-77.

concubine became the mistress and her children bastards'.[82]

The thesis of Goody's book is that all these changes came about – the banning by the church of close-kin marriages, levirate marriage, adoption and concubinage – because the church needed to create the situation in which property owners were left without heirs and were therefore more likely to leave their property to the church. His argument is that the social arrangements that were banned had functioned socially to ensure that property was inherited within the narrow family kin group. However, the development of a church with celibate clergy and monastic communities, all of which needed to be financed by those who had not embraced the clerical or monastic professions, required the destruction of the social mechanisms that kept property within the narrower family. If this was achieved, heirless property owners would be more likely to dispose of their wealth to the church and religious foundations.[83]

Whether or not Goody's argument is valid as an explanation of the changes introduced by the church, there is no doubt that, from at least the fourth century A.D., the monastic way of life was considered to be the superior way of being a follower of Jesus Christ. Mention has also been made earlier of the importance of Virgins – women who deliberately opted for celibacy in order to devote themselves to Christian work. It must not be forgotten that early Christianity presented radical alternatives to the ways in which

---

[82] Goody, *Development*, p.77.
[83] Goody, *Development*, p.46 and *passim*..

family life had been envisaged and practised previously, and that these alternatives were believed to be sanctioned by the life and example of Jesus and the teaching of Paul.

Godparents
Another radical innovation in Christian practice was spiritual kinship in general, including godparenting in particular, although Goody points out that blood-brotherhood and forms of quasi-kinship are found in many societies.[84] In Christian practice, sponsorship at Baptism developed into god-parenting. Apparently, at some periods of the church's history, spiritual kinship could function as a bar to marriage.

Goody draws attention to certain features of the Book of Common Prayer regarding godparenting, which appear in a new light when considered in the context of the history of spiritual kinship in the church. The Baptism service implies that the child has been brought to the church by the godparents, not the parents. It is to the former, not the latter, that the priest says:
> *Dearly beloved, ye have brought this Child here to be baptised.*

A later rubric says
> *Then shall the Priest take the Child into his hands, and shall say to the Godfathers and Godmothers, Name this Child.*

Following the Baptism, the godparents are exhorted to ensure that the child is brought up

---

[84] Goody, *Development*, p.194 and the whole chapter 'The spiritual and the natural' pp.194-221.

christianly, and presented in due course to the bishop for Confirmation. In the Catechism the Candidate is asked for his or her name. 'Who gave you this name?' The reply is 'My Godfathers and Godmothers in my Baptism'. It may be that a change in the function and status of the godparent can be discerned from a comparison of the rubrics at the end of the Catechism in the 1549 and 1552 Books of Common Prayer on the one hand, and that in the 1662 book on the other. The earlier books have

> *then shall they be broughte to the Bishop by one that shalbe hys Godfather, or Godmother that every childe maye have a witnes of his confirmacion.*

The 1662 Book has
> *every one shall have a Godfather, or a Godmother, as a witness of their Confirmation.*

It has been suggested that the earlier wording implies the custom of having a new godparent at Confirmation, a custom that was dying out in 1662.[85] What is striking to a modern reader is the complete lack of reference to *parents* in the Catechism and Baptism services of the Prayer Books from 1549 to 1662. The implication of this may be, of course, no more than that it had become customary for children to be baptised as soon as possible after birth, which for obvious reasons precluded the mother from attending, and by extension, the father. Also, the mother would not be expected to appear in church until she had

---

[85] W.K.L.Clarke, 'Confirmation' in W.K.L.Clarke (ed.) *Liturgy and Worship. A Companion to the Prayer Books of the Anglican Communion.* London: SPCK, 1932. p.452.

been 'churched' 'at the usual time after her delivery'.[86] If she was unmarried she was also required to do penance before being 'churched', a subject that we address in the final chapter.[87]

The Continental Reformers
The Continental Reformers rejected the norms that had been established in the pre-Reformation church and especially the way in which the church had hitherto interpreted the prohibitions on sexual liaisons in Leviticus 18 and 20. Luther regarded the system in place in his day as a way of raising money, because the prohibitions were such that they required many dispensations, for which fees had to be paid. Luther argued that only those liaisons that were explicitly mentioned in Leviticus 18 and 20 were prohibited as opposed to the then practice of working from degrees of marriage. He pointed out that the Bible forbade marriage with an aunt, but failed to mention a niece, although she would be related to a man in the same degree as his aunt (in fact, the man's grandfather would be his niece's great-grandfather, and his aunt's uncle).[88] Luther argued that the Bible forbade marriage with a step-child, a degree allowed today by the Church of England but forbidden by the Church in Wales.[89] Luther also allowed the marriage of a

---

[86] Book of Common Prayer, prefatory rubric to the Thanksgiving of Women after Child-birth.
[87] F. Procter, W.H. Frere, *A New History of The Book of Common Prayer. With a Rationale of its Offices*, London: Macmillan, 3rd. ed 1905, p. 640 note 5.
[88] M. Luther, *Luther's Works*, vol.45, Philadelphia: Muhlenberg Press, 1962, p.23. See further J.W.Rogerson, *According to the Scriptures?*, pp.54-5.
[89] Beesley, *Anglican Marriage*, p.46.

man to his deceased wife's sister, a relationship considered by the Church of England, for most of its history, to be forbidden by the Bible, and only allowed by the Canon Law of the church after the Second World War. The history of this and related legislation shows how attitudes to marriage relationships have changed in the course of time.

Attempts to change the law to allow a man to marry his deceased wife's sister were made early in the 19th century, and according to F.W. Cornish the effect of an Act of 1835 was to legitimise 'connexions [i.e. deceased wife's sister marriages] which had been entered into in all grades of society, and which were looked upon by those who had contracted them as lawful marriages'.[90] The Act declared that any future marriages within this relationship would be null and void. A bill to allow such marriages was introduced in 1883 and successfully opposed by the Church even though Queen Victoria supported it strongly.[91] Finally, a bill introduced in 1907 passed successfully into law despite opposition from the Church of England and from this point until after the Second World War Statute Law was at variance with Canon Law.[92] Acts to legitimise marriage with a deceased brother's widow and with nieces and nephews by marriage were passed in 1921 and 1931, the former to compensate for the shortage of men following the First World War. It is

---

[90] F.W. Cornish, *A History of the English Church in the Nineteenth Century*, London: Macmillan & Co., Part II, 1910, pp. 93-95. The Act of 1835 was Lord Lyndhurst's Act, a private Act brought to legitimise the noble Lord's own marriage!

[91] G. K.A. Bell, *Randall Davidson, Archbishop of Canterbury*, London: Oxford University Press, 3rd ed. 1952, p. 96.

[92] Bell, *Randall Davidson*, 550-556.

interesting to compare the arguments that were advanced by the Church against the proposed legislation at that time with those that are at present raised against same-sex marriage.

Richard Baxter's position
The Puritan divine Richard Baxter (1615-1691), wrote at a time when the Old Testament had been largely rehabilitated in England as a source for guidance for Christians. His *Christian Directory*, compiled in 1664-5 and published in 1673, is a monumental work covering every conceivable aspect of Christian living.[93] Baxter represents seventeenth-century Puritan theology at its best, combining a profound knowledge of Protestant scholastic learning with an openness to rational thought that sometimes makes him appear 'liberal' compared with twenty-first century conservative evangelicals.[94] What cannot be questioned was his commitment to the Bible as divinely inspired revelation.

Baxter, who married in 1662 shortly before compiling the *Christian Directory*, defined the family as follows: 'we mean, not a tribe or stock of kinship… but I mean a household'.[95] While noting that a household had four internal parts: father, mother, son, and servant, Baxter allowed that the essence of a family was 'one head or governor, either father, mother, master, or mistress; and one

---

[93] R. Baxter, *The Practical Works of Richard Baxter. 1 A Christian Directory*, Morgan, PA: Soli Deo Gloria Publications, 2000.
[94] See Rogerson, *According to the Scriptures?*, pp.66-72.
[95] Baxter, *Directory*, p.410.

or more governed under this head'.[96] He justified this understanding of the family by reference to Old Testament texts such as Joshua 24.15 'But as for me and my house, we will serve the LORD' as well as examples from Acts:16.14-15 (Lydia and her household are baptised), 16.33-34 (baptism of the Philippian gaoler and his house) and 18.8 (Crispus and his house are baptised). Whether or not a man should marry and establish a family was essentially a matter between the believer and God. Baxter appreciated fully what he considered to be the advantages of not marrying, referring to Paul's teaching in 1 Corinthians 7.7-8, 32-35 (ideally, Paul's readers should remain as they are, i.e. not marry if they are single, because single people can devote themselves more fully to the service of God) and urged caution on those contemplating marriage. 'Let the holy fear of God be preferred in your choice... Marry not a swine for a golden trough, nor an ugly soul for a comely body'.[97]

In laying down guidelines for what a Christian family should look like, Baxter referred to many biblical passages. Deuteronomy 6.6-7 ('these words... shall be upon your heart; and you shall teach them diligently to your children') expected parents to instruct children in the ways of God, Ecclesiastes 4.9-12 ('two are better than one...') outlined the benefits of mutual support of husband and wife, while the behaviour of the sons of Eli in 1 Samuel 3.13 (they blasphemed God) gave an example to be avoided. Adultery was an offence that carried the death penalty in the Old

---

[96] Baxter, *Directory*, p.410.
[97] Baxter, *Directory*, p.402

Testament (Baxter cited Leviticus 20.10) and was a ground for the wronged innocent party to seek a divorce. Baxter wrote strongly against any behaviour in which the need to satisfy human lust threatened the marriage covenant, and he referred to a whole battery of texts from all parts of the Bible in support.[98]

He considered a number of legal points. Could a person marry against the wishes of parents? What if parents or a prince ordered a person to marry against his will? Could parents order the dissolution of a marriage of which they did not approve if sexual relations had not yet taken place? Could the aged who were 'uncapable (sic) of procreation' marry? Suppose a woman had made a vow to someone to marry him, could disapproving parents declare the vow to be invalid? How were the provisions of Leviticus 18 to be applied (a) if the state allowed close relatives to marry which Leviticus forbade, (b) if it forbade close relatives to marry which Leviticus allowed? What about the marriage of [first] cousins? Baxter dealt with all these and similar questions in a balanced manner, mixed with firmness and generosity. The marriage of [first] cousins was not prohibited by Scripture, and the children of Noah's sons must have married their cousins, because there was no other possibility. Indeed, the sons of Adam and Eve must have married their sisters for the same reason, and if people constrained by 'natural necessity;' such as a man and his sister 'cast alone upon a foreign wilderness' felt that God wished them to increase

---

[98] Baxter, *Directory*, p.432, footnote b.

and multiply' they could, in Baxter's view, lawfully marry.[99]

An interesting use of the Old Testament was made in regard to the question whether parents could annul a vow made by a daughter. Baxter referred to Numbers 30.3-5 (which he inaccurately cited as the third chapter of Numbers). Here, it is laid down that if a woman, within her father's house and in her youth, makes a vow, the vow can stand if the father hears of it and says nothing at the time. Only if he expresses disapproval on the day that he hears it is the vow invalid. The continuation of the passage, in Numbers 30.6-15, applies the law similarly in cases where a married woman makes a vow and her husband hears of it. On the matters of parental permission or parental command, Baxter affirmed the duty of children to obey their parents but outlined situations in which this duty was not absolute. An overriding consideration was the salvation of an individual and the work of the gospel. Baxter affirmed the right of an aged person beyond the age of procreation to marry. If the state allowed marriage among close relatives not permitted by Scripture, the Bible had to be obeyed and marriage with the close relatives avoided.

'Content' and 'form' of marriage
One point that emerges strongly from Baxter's discussion is that although the *form* of marriage and the family is important, its *content* is more important. Much space is devoted to outlining the

---

[99] Baxter, *Directory*, p.405.

duties of spouses to each other and to their children, and of the duties of children to their parents. The family, as a household, is seen as a microcosm of the people of God, whose vocation is to be holy in the many practical senses of this notion.

If we take the idea of *content* as more important than *form* back to the Bible we find a good deal of disturbing material. The family of Isaac is 'regular' in form (he has only one wife, Rebekah) but far from harmonious in content. His younger son, Jacob, tricks his brother Esau out of his birthright and then, with the connivance of Rebekah, deceives Isaac into giving him the blessing properly reserved for Esau. The deception involves not only the economically unacceptable killing of two kids from the flock, but deliberate lying in God's name by Jacob (Genesis 27.5-29). When Jacob takes refuge from Esau with his uncle Laban's family in distant Haran, he repays the hospitality that he receives with further dishonesty. He waits until Laban is shearing his sheep and departs for the land of Canaan taking flocks and offspring that technically are Laban's property, together with Laban's household gods, which may also have been title deeds to property (Genesis 31). Previously, he had been treated dishonestly when Laban gave him Leah as a wife when Jacob had been promised her younger sister Rachel (Genesis 29). The family of David, albeit not 'regular' in form (i.e. it was not monogamous) was also dysfunctional, with Tamar raped by a half-brother, and Tamar's brother Absalom having the culprit, Amnon, murdered (2 Samuel 13). On the other hand, families that are 'unusual' can be the site of conspicuous loyalty. After a series of misfortunes the immediate family of Naomi consists of only herself and her Moabite daughter-in-law, Ruth. Yet Ruth displays a degree of loyalty to Naomi that is one of the high points of the Old Testament, as she declares that she will never abandon her mother-in-law (Ruth 1.16-17). Another notable narrative is that of the relationship between David and Saul's son Jonathan (1 Samuel 18.1-5). This results in Jonathan showing a loyalty to David that overrides Jonathan's obligations to his father, Saul. When Saul wishes to kill David, Jonathan warns David not to attend a new-year feast (1 Samuel 20. 18-42. David later adopts Jonathan's son in order to show kindness 'for Jonathan's sake' (2 Samuel 9.1-8).

The consideration of the *content* of family life raises a fundamental question. Is the *form* of a family more important than its *content*? Is it better for a family to be 'regular' in the sense that it conforms to the traditional interpretation of Genesis 2.23-4 even if its behaviour falls well below standards of honesty and decency, than for a family to be irregular from the point of view of Genesis 2.23-4 as traditionally understood even if its behaviour is admirable? Is the 'regular' family of Isaac and Rebekah with its scheming sons 'better' than the 'irregular' family of Elkanah who has two wives but who shows especial love to Hannah who is childless (1 Samuel 1.1-8)? What about the conduct of Abram, who at the time of the narrative has only one wife, and the monogamous Isaac, both of whom deny that they have a wife, when they feel that their lives are threatened when foreign rulers with whom they have taken refuge wish to take their wives into the harem (Genesis 12.1-20, 26.6-16)? Is it creditable behaviour for them to abandon their wives in order to save themselves? It must also be noted that some of the prophets in the Old Testament (not to mention Paul in the New Testament!) remain unmarried. This is apparently the case with Elijah and Elisha, while Jeremiah is explicitly commanded not to take a wife (Jeremiah 16.2).

Karl Barth's contribution to the discussion
At this point another theologian will be considered who cannot be accused of being indifferent to the Bible any more than Baxter can be, and whose thinking takes up these problems and puts them into a new perspective. I refer here to Karl Barth's *Kirchliche Dogmatik* (*Church Dogmatics*) and to volume III/4 published in 1957[100] What is important about Barth's use of the Bible is his insistence that it is not a law book but the Word of God witnessing to the grace of God revealed in Jesus Christ. Barth insists that it is necessary to think biblically not legally.[101] What this means is that passages in the Bible about men and women, marriage and the family, must be read inter-textually (as we would say today) and in the context of the revelation of God's grace. The human race is confronted by God's commandment. This commandment cannot be confined to any one particular biblical passage. It

---
[100] K. Barth, *Kirchliche Dogmatik*, Bd.III *Die Lehre von der Schöpfung*, Vierter Teil, Zollikon-Zürich: Evangelischer Verlag, 1957.
[101] Barth, *Kirchliche Dogmatik* III/4 p.223.

embraces and transcends particular passages at the same time that particular passages express aspects of the commandment. The commandment limits and defines the human race, but also offers freedom. This freedom comes from the fact that the commandment is **God's** commandment and therefore an expression of his concern with and for the human race. The freedom is also bound up with the fact that because Jesus has fulfilled the commandment, those (and that is everyone) who fall short are offered forgiveness and hope in the name of Jesus.

God's commandment to the human race is that people should be what they are, namely, men and women, with those things that make up their distinctive being as men and women. (Barth describes homosexuality as an illness (*Krankheit*), although he appears to make no distinction between homosexual orientation and homosexual activity.)[102] Men and women taken together constitute humanity in its fullness and completeness. Marriage is a special and unique form of relationship between men and women, something that affects their lives as a whole. Barth strongly criticises the idea that any one aspect of married life, for example, sexual activity, should be singled out as having special importance. Marriage is a voluntary response to the commandment of God understood in its broadest sense. This commandment does not rule out celibacy or (a common Protestant view) deem it to be inferior to marriage. It does not assume that the purpose of marriage is to produce children and a family. The commandment establishes an

---

[102] Barth, *Kirchliche Dogmatik* III/4 p.184.

order (*Ordnung*) in which a man and a woman are called into a life-partnership (*Lebensgemeinschaft*) and given the task (*Aufgabe*) of being human in accordance with God's will and purpose.

This approach leads to some interesting interpretations of biblical passages. Genesis 2.24, 'therefore a man leaves his father and his mother and cleaves to his wife and they become one flesh' has traditionally been interpreted in a sexual sense. Not so Barth. Apart from the fact that such an interpretation lays emphasis on one aspect of marriage to the exclusion of others, it makes no sense of the whole of the biblical message. Here, Barth pays particular attention to Ephesians 5.32, where Genesis 2.24 is interpreted to refer to 'Christ and the church'. From this, Barth argues that in the Old Testament the union between man and woman described in Genesis 2.24 must be understood in terms of the bond between God and his Chosen People in establishing his covenant with them.[103] Against the interpretation of Genesis 2.24 in physical sexual terns Barth considers 1 Corinthians 6.16 and Ephesians 5.31. His argument rests, perhaps tenuously, on the fact that when Paul says in the 1 Corinthians passage that a man who joins himself to a prostitute becomes one body with her, the Greek word used is *sôma*. The quotation from Genesis 2.24 is from the Greek translation of the Old Testament where 'one flesh' uses the Greek word *sarx* (similarly Ephesians 5.31). Barth maintains that the use of the two words *sôma* and *sarx* shows that the

---

[103] Barth, *KD* III/4 p.158.

passage does not refer exclusively to the physical-sexual aspects of being human. They include those aspects, but the reference is to the total and inclusive commonality (*Gemeinsamkeit*) or inclusiveness of interests, of the two people.[104]

Barth's comments on the family are equally interesting.[105]. Noting that a family in the Old and New Testaments was a household, Barth argues that from a total biblical perspective, the only importance that the families described in the Old Testament have is that they are part of the Chosen People into which Christ is born. In the New Testament the family has no importance. Leading figures are identified not in terms of their families or parents, but in terms of their places of origin: Jesus of Nazareth, Judas man of Kerioth (Iscariot), Simon of Cyrene, Saul of Tarsus. 'It was only habitual ways of thinking and the practical conventions of the "christianised" Gentiles, that gave the notion of the family the lustre of a fundamental term of Christian ethics. We have no cause to follow them'.[106]

Barth's approach opens up a number of possibilities for questions that concern the present book. First, he makes a distinction that is difficult to translate into English between *Heirat* and *Ehe*, both of which are normally rendered as 'marriage'

---

[104] Barth, *KD*, III/4, p.148.
[105] Barth, *KD*, III/4, p.270-1
[106] Barth, *KD*, III/4, p.271, 'Es waren Denkgewohnheiten und praktische Gepflogenheiten der „christianisierten"
Heidenvölker, die dem Begriff „Familie" später den Glanz eines Grundbegriffes christlicher Ethik gegeben haben. Wir haben keinen Anlaß, uns ihnen anzuschließen'.

in English. By *Heirat* he means a properly legally constituted marriage bond. By *Ehe* he means the condition of two people living under and according to God's commandment. The former does not necessarily coincide with the latter. Two people can be married legally (*Heirat*), but not living in a way that could be called marriage (*Ehe*). Again, two people could be not married (in the legal sense) and yet (precariously for Barth) be living in a relationship that could be called *Ehe*.[107] Barth also allows that in missionary situations, where the Gospel is received by a society in which polygamy is an institution, it is not impossible that a polygamous relationship could be a marriage (*Ehe*) truly under God's commandment.[108].

Barth, by his biblical rather than legal approach to the use of the Bible, has opened up some interesting possibilities. Before these are outlined however, it must be said in fairness to Barth that he would most probably have disagreed with the way that matters of family and parental responsibility have developed in English law. Barth died in 1968 and it is obviously foolish to speculate on what he might have thought about civil partnerships and fertility treatment involving donors and surrogacy. The logic of his position and statements in the *Church Dogmatics* would be against these developments. If he regarded homosexuality as an illness (*Krankheit*) he could hardly approve of two men or two women entering into a civil partnership. His only reference to artificial insemination comes in a

---

[107] Barth, *KD*, III/4, p.253.
[108] Barth, *KD* III/4, p.237.

comment on Aldous Huxley's *Brave New World*, a book which he describes as *schrecklich* (frightful, or dreadful); and his point that there can be no third party in a marriage would appear to rule out surrogacy and donor insemination.[109] There is also his point that marriage is not or should not be primarily entered into in order to beget children. This would presumably rule out any suggestion that a childless couple had a 'right' to medical treatment designed to help them produce offspring. A more recent discussion of these issues from a German Protestant viewpoint firmly rules out egg donation or donor insemination.[110] It is argued that the possibilities raised by the various different combinations of 'natural' and non-natural parents will lead to the 'dissolution of the family' (*die Auflösung der Familie*) although 'family' is not defined in the discussion. However, employing Barth's arguments in ways of which he might not have approved, it can be said that what matters is not the *form* of a relationship but its *content*; that, in theory at any rate, a family defined in terms of a household whose members are not in 'regular' relationships might fulfil the aims of mutual love and support more adequately than a family whose parents are legally married with naturally-produced children.

---

[109] Barth, *KD*, III/4, p.449 for the comments on Huxley; p.218 for the insistence that there can be no third party.
[110] M. Honecker, *Grundriß der Sozialethik*, Berlin: de Gruyter, 1995, pp.111-2. The Roman Catholic Church takes a similar line.

> ## Discussion points
> Two questions for discussion in groups:
> 1. What is marriage for?
> If it is for more than the legal/moral containment of sex, or for the purposes of having legitimate children, what other purposes does it serve?
>
> 2. Can a family be a group not related by blood or marriage? Can you suggest some examples?

Chapter 7
Using the Bible today
by J W Rogerson
& Imogen Clout

Suggestions about how we can use the Bible and apply its teachings to modern life

---

The aim of what has been written so far has not been to 'baptise', so to speak, the relationships and arrangements that now exist as possibilities in English law. Given that civil partnerships between male couples and female couples exist, and that co-habiting same-sex couples share certain legal rights with them in matters of parental responsibility; and given that children can be born to heterosexual and same-sex couples by surrogacy and sperm-donor arrangements as regulated by law, how is the Bible to be read today in the light of these arrangements? There will be various possible answers.

Precept or example?
One answer, based upon an interpretation of Genesis 2.24 and backed by an interpretation of Jesus's reference to it at Mark 10.7, will be that any deviation from 'one man one woman for life' is against the teaching of the Bible. The text says nothing about surrogacy, of course.

A different answer would be that Old Testament society was polygamous, that men called by God to be kings and leaders of the nation had more than one wife without divine censure, and that Genesis 2.24 cannot, therefore, be referring to monogamous marriage. This answer would also draw attention to stories about surrogacy in the Bible (Hagar for Abraham, Zilhah and Bilhah for Jacob and Ruth and Boaz for Naomi) as well as the provision of levirate marriage. This approach would not necessarily endorse the various possibilities of relationship and procreation now enshrined in English law, but it would question whether such a hard-line approach as in the first answer was a responsible use of the Bible.

A fundamental question, which Barth's use of the Bible raises, is whether the Bible exists to be a lawbook, or whether its purpose is to witness to God's revelation in Jesus Christ. This is another way of viewing the distinction between the letter and the spirit, a distinction that goes back to Paul (2 Corinthians3.6). It is also a way of asking the question whether the *form* of relationship is more important than its *content*.

Any insistence that there has, from the beginning, been one and one only Christian pattern of family life, based upon the Bible, that this pattern must be maintained at all costs, and that any alternatives or deviations from this pattern would be contrary to the teaching of the Bible, must be rejected. It may well be that what some wrongly regard as the one and only pattern ('one man, one woman for life') has many good features, such as the ideal that marriage should be a life-long commitment. However, the fact is that there have been a number of varying patterns of what constitutes Christian family life, and the Bible has been used both to support and to reject aspects of these patterns. Second, legal frameworks regulating marriage and families have been especially designed with property and inheritance in view. If Goody is correct, the intention at one stage was to divert property from families to the church and monastic foundations. From the Reformation onwards there was a move back towards ensuring that property was inherited within families. Some modern legislation, e.g. regarding civil partnerships, has been aimed at enabling same-sex couples to enjoy the same inheritance rights as heterosexual couples. This aspect of family law should not be neglected in modern discussions. It surely cannot be at variance with Christian and biblical principles that legal frameworks should be established whose aim is to ensure fair treatment in matters of property and inheritance to all people, whatever their sexual orientations and how they express them.

Structures of grace
John has argued elsewhere that the Bible helps us in social and moral questions not by precept but by example:[111] not by requiring us to adopt those few and diminishing precepts from the Bible that can be transferred without remainder to today's western industrialised society, but by showing how imperatives of redemption resulted in the Old Testament in the urging of structures of grace - practical arrangements designed to encourage

---

[111] Rogerson, *According to the Scriptures?* pp.80-86.

graciousness. An excellent example comes in Deuteronomy 15.12-18 in connection with the release of slaves after they have served for six years. The master who is releasing his slave is enjoined to furnish him liberally out of his flock, his threshing floor and his wine press. 'As the LORD your God has blessed you, you shall give to him' (verse 14). This is not legislation in the strict sense. It is an appeal to the generosity and creativity of the master. It is asking him to recognise that if the slave is to make his way independently, he needs resources to be given a start. This structure of grace is grounded in the following imperative of redemption: 'You shall remember that you were a slave in Egypt, and the LORD your God redeemed you; therefore I command you this today' (verse 15). It cannot be applied directly today. Slavery has been abolished, officially at any rate. We can say, of course, that the passage is irrelevant because the situation it addresses no longer exists. Alternatively, we can say that the passage gives us an example to follow: to ask whether there are situations over which we have some control and are challenged to use our imagination and generosity to devise structures that will extend graciousness to others.

Various forms of marriage and family life have been structures of grace in Christian history. Virginity enabled women to escape from the domination of patriarchal households so that they could devote themselves to Christian service. The monastic life enabled people to organise hospitals, and care for the sick and elderly, or to enable research and teaching to be carried out. No doubt traditional marriages have also often been structures of grace for parents, children and wider families. In our view, the churches should approach the changes happening in contemporary society not with a thou-shalt-not attitude, but seeking to see how they might be helped to be structures of grace. Such an approach does not, of course, simply endorse everything that is proposed. A structure of grace has no room for injustice or intolerance and can be critical as well as affirmative.

The overriding question that we have to face is whether the task of the churches is primarily to regulate the structures in which family life is organised, or whether their task is primarily to preach and make available the gospel of the grace and mercy of God revealed in Jesus Christ. If a biblical example is needed at this point, that of Paul is surely paramount. In the semi-autobiographical passage in Philippians 3, Paul described the institutions which had shaped his life before he became a follower of Jesus. He was a circumcised Hebrew, of the tribe of Benjamin, a Pharisee, and a strict observer of the law, a law that he regarded as revealed by God. Yet he was prepared to give up all these things, and the privileges that went with them, for the sake of Christ. 'For his sake I have suffered the loss of all things, and count them as refuse, in order that I may gain Christ (verse 8). The Greek word translated here as 'refuse' (*dzemia*) is rendered as 'garbage' in the New English Bible. A modern colloquial equivalent might be 'shit'. This meant that Paul was willing to teach that non-Jews who became Christians were not obliged to observe the law, the law that he believed had been revealed by God.

There is an important passage in 1 Corinthians 9.19-23.

For though I am free from all men, I have made myself a slave to all, that I might win the more. To the Jews I became as a Jew, in order to win Jews; to those under the law I became as one under the law – though not being myself under the law – that I might win those under the law. To those outside the law I became as one outside the law - not being without law toward God but under the law of Christ – that I might win those outside the law. To the weak I became weak, that I might win the weak. I have become all things to all men, that I might by all means save some. I do it all for the sake of the gospel.

Commenting on this passage C.K. Barrett wrote: *'It is true and important that, as recent research has emphasized, Paul remained in many respects not merely a Jew but a Pharisee and a Rabbi: yet he differed from all non-Christian Pharisees in that he was ready (in the interests of the Gospel...) to cease to be a Jew'.*[112]

One might adapt this statement to the needs of the present book in the following way. The church exists to uphold traditional forms of the family insofar as these provide for long-term faithfulness between spouses, and loving relationships between parents and children, but it is ready, in the interests of the Gospel, to welcome those for whom traditional forms do not meet their needs, insofar as these alternatives provide

---

[112] C.K. Barrett, *The First Epistle to the Corinthians* (Black's New Testament Commentaries), London: Adam & Charles Black, 1968, p.211.

for long-term faithfulness and loving situations in which children can be nurtured.

Looking at the quality of relationships
We suggest that it may be helpful for the Church to reconsider family life, not in terms of what might be seen as the biological and legal structures of families, but instead looking at emotional relationships and responsibilities. This would mean that we concentrate instead on parents and the parental role in relationships. Our present tendency is to analyse a family like this: "a lesbian couple (are they civil partners?) with one child from each of their previous relationships, so they are both step-parents and they've had another child, together – (which one was the 'real' mother?)". Imagine a different approach: here are two people, obviously in a loving and committed relationship, and they are bringing up three children, whom they love.

If we get away from the biology, if we leave the question of the parents' sexual relationship out of our considerations, and the judgement that we might be tempted to vent about why they chose to have a child, we can concentrate on the fact that they are lovingly raising children in a stable household. This is a good thing. This is a structure of grace. Being a parent to a child – and we include all people who raise children, their own or other people's in that broad sense – is a mighty act of love. It calls for patience, humour, kindness, sacrifice, firmness and altruism. It has marvellous compensations too.

If the legal concept of what being a parent entails has shifted and widened from the facts of birth and adoption to the concept of Parental Responsibility, a status which can be held by many more people that the original biological parents, the Church can learn from this. The Church has tended to neglect the idea of being a parent, as opposed to being a mother or a father. It's a comparatively modern concept. The idea of "parenting", both as a skill, or action and even using the word as verb is a modern concept, which might have puzzled our forefathers (and mothers).

The 1974 edition of the Shorter Oxford English Dictionary does not give a usage of 'parent' as a verb, and this accords with our recollection of first encountering someone using it in the early 1980s, and recoiling slightly at the idea of using the noun as a verb. Now we see it used everywhere: parenting classes and courses are widely available. It is accepted that it is a skill that can be learned or enhanced. It seems that the use of the verb 'to parent' fills a gap that we needed as we have come to think about what being a parent involves.

What did we say before we said "to parent"? To "mother" has particular overtones of caring, nurturing. It implies a closeness and physicality, a softness and gentleness. To "father" has a completely different feel. "Fathering" a child simply connotes the act of procreation – after that the child, and by association, the mother, are on their own. Loving, caring fathers will feel that this is unfair. There isn't a helpful word that really describes the role that they play in their children's lives as they grow up. Then we come to words that do not connote who is doing the action: to rear, to bring up, to raise. "Bring up" is probably the term that was most often used in our youth. Oh, the disapproval that could be conveyed by the phrase "badly brought up"!

Using 'parent' as a verb does give us a gender-neutral word that allows both parents to have a role in upbringing, and suggests that what they bring to the role is specific to their relationship with the child: a bond of caring created by love and dependence.

The heart of Jesus' teaching was the image of God as parent, an unconditionally loving father. This is the key image of the parable that so many generations have known as 'The Prodigal Son'. It should so much more be called 'The Loving Father'. God as parent in the New Testament is the loving parent whom Jesus calls by the intimate name 'Abba'. Unfortunately people often conflate the loving father with the apparently rather sterner God we meet in the Old Testament. However, when we meet God as a parent in the Old Testament (and there are only a few references, and God is often a mother) that image is always used of God in a loving, tender relationship with his or her people.

Instead of using the holy family as a model for a tiny (respectable) nuclear family, let us think about the real implications of the way that Jesus was brought up. If we analysed the Holy Family in the censorious way that we described above, how might you categorise them?
"Vast difference in age – she's young enough to be his daughter – pregnant before they got married – not clear who the father is – could be a surrogate

baby – not sure whether he's going to adopt it or not – and what about all those stepchildren? [113] – how's she going to manage?"

Turn the analysis around, and concentrate on the parents' relationship with the children. Both Mary and Joseph must have been exceptionally loving for Jesus to have turned out as he did. He spoke of love from first hand. He knew how a really loving father behaves. He modelled this love to his followers. He managed his diverse group of disciples with love, and humour and good temper and rigour. He made them into a family, and he did it so well that after his death his family could go on with the pattern of life that he had taught them.

So it should not be too radical a step to bring the focus of our thinking about the family onto the way adults care for children, or the stronger and older care for the weaker and younger, and both generations learn from each other. Not only is this a better way of helping us to look at individual families, it also gives us a way of thinking about that glibly used cliché, 'the family of the Church'. We all have parental roles that we can exercise to each other, in the way we care for and teach each other about the world. This is an important part of our life in church communities, one of the few social organisations where generations meet and mix. People who have never been biological parents can have a parental role to others, and not always those

---

[113] If you take the view that the 'brothers and sisters' mentioned in Matthew must have come from Joseph's first marriage

younger than themselves. It is also a great grace to accept that you may be in the role of a child and allow someone else to be parental towards you.

Unfortunately there is a tendency in some congregations to think that the 'family of the Church' metaphor is fulfilled by putting the priest in the parental role – Father so-and-so – and for the rest of the congregation to be the children. The ambiguities of the fatherly role in this context have been exposed by women coming into the priesthood. Some balk at being called 'Mother' and opt for 'Father' instead. This implies that the title 'Father' is more about authority and control than loving parenthood. Many priests are also rather vexed at what they feel is a tendency in their congregations to behave not so much as children as infants, with a sort of feeble deference that refuses to assume responsibility.

If we think seriously about what being a parent involves, it must be clear that children *grow up,* and good parenting is about how you manage and nurture that change. You do not keep your children in a state of dependent infantilism, you teach them and feed them and *bring them up.* You accept that they will reach maturity and you do everything that you can to help them get to the point where they will not need you as much. And you will still love them and hope that they go on loving you, not out of need but mutual affection.

New and remerging patters of family life need to be supported or sustained by appropriate ceremonies that express the reality of family life and celebrate its structure of grace. This is the subject of Chapter 8.

Discussion points

Consider the references to God as parent (whether mother or father) in the Old Testament, and what overall model of parenting that might create

Deuteronomy 8, 5
Deuternomy 32, 11
Deuteronomy 32, 18
Job 38, 28-29
Psalm 103,13
Proverbs 3, 11-12
Isaiah 1, 1-4
Isaiah 30, 1
Isaiah 49, 14-15
Isaiah 54, 5-8
Isaiah 62, 4-5
Isaiah 64, 8
Isaiah 66, 13
Jeremiah 31, 9 and 20
Hosea 11, 1 - 4
Malachi 1, 6
Malachi 3, 17

Chapter 8

Customs and ceremonies

by J W Rogerson

& Imogen Clout

How creating and using new liturgies and customs can help create a welcome for all families

---

> *A story from Imogen's family.*
> *Imogen's mother's grandmother grew up on a fairly isolated farm in Cheshire in the 1860s. Family tradition tells that in their household whenever they set the farmhouse table for a meal they always set an extra place, just in case someone should call unexpectedly. This is the essence of hospitality: the conscious practical readiness to welcome a guest, whoever they are, and to share whatever the family has at table.*

In this part of the chapter we want to consider the liturgies that are provided by churches for the significant times of family life. Do they meet the needs of the people for whom they are designed? Do they, by implication extend the hospitality of the Church? And are there other aspects of family life that are neglected and could do with more official liturgical support?

In suggesting revised and new liturgies we would not want to fetter the creative impulse of the minister who is a skilled liturgist, ready to create services and prayers to serve specific needs of his or her congregation or parish. There will always be the place for the tailor-made prayer or rite. Many ministers, however, are not skilled at liturgy and in any event are busy, with many calls on their time, so they cannot be expected to produce services to order. Further, if such prayers and rites are already in the repertoire, their existence is evidence of the hospitality and welcome of the Church, just as the setting of the extra place at the table makes someone feel a welcome guest, not a burden.

Imagine a family, perhaps a same-sex couple who have just had a baby using a fertility clinic, or a step-family where the step-father has just acquired parental responsibility for the children, approaching their vicar, to ask (probably rather tentatively) if this new family structure can be recognised in some way. How will they feel if the vicar is taken aback and gives a response like this: 'well, this is quite unusual, we'll have to adapt something for you'. Contrast that with the way that it would feel if they were told that there is a service in the book that has already been designed with them in mind. Most of us, however individual we like to feel we are, also want the reassurance of being told that we are 'normal' and the acceptance that goes with this.

What is liturgy for?
A detailed examination of the power and purpose of liturgy is not within the scope of this book. We

should, however, consider what we think liturgy is for and what it does.

Liturgy should move us, by its use of words, their rhetorical ordering and pace, by its use of gesture and symbol, into a state of emotional, spiritual and intellectual response to God. Good liturgy will uplift us, warm our hearts (strangely, as John Wesley had it), comfort and strengthen us. It has the power to jolt us into new ways of thinking, and to heal us. It is probably more important that it works on our emotions than our intellects, but it needs both. Words recalled in tranquillity, when emotion may have faded, need to stand up to scrutiny and not be revealed as shallow and trite.

Liturgy that is repeated daily or weekly, so that it is understood by heart, by a regular congregation, has its own particular features. The liturgy of the occasional offices, which we are considering in this chapter, has to fulfil a different purpose. Most of those at the service may have never heard these words before, so it is important that they have an immediate impact; that they are accessible, but not bland. They also need power and warmth, so that they sound as though they really matter, and are not a series of religious clichés strung together. They need too to be poetic: that is, they need to work on more than one metaphorical level, so that they engage the imagination, and give pleasure. We should be aware that liturgy works both at a conscious level and also, deeper, on our unspoken subconscious.

Let us look then, at the services in the repertoire of the Church that do deal with the significant events of family life, and consider how they might need sensitive adaptation to meet the needs of all modern families.

We will start with the Churching of Women, no longer a service in regular use, and dropped from ASB and Common Worship. It was replaced by various forms of Thanksgivings for children, which, we will argue, changed the nature of the service, forgetting its original purpose. Thanksgivings, in their turn, have blurred into Baptisms, and we need to think clearly about what the purpose of each is, and what we think are the effects of such liturgies.

The Churching of Women
Up to the Second World War it was a common practice for a woman who had given birth[114] to come to her parish church about six weeks later and be ceremonially received back into her community. The short service of thanksgiving assumed that the woman had survived a perilous ordeal. The words of the appointed Psalm, 116, make this clear:

'The snares of death compassed me round about: and the pains of hell gat hold upon me.
I found trouble and heaviness and I called upon the name of the Lord….
….I was in misery and he helped me…
Thou hast delivered my soul from death: mine eyes from tears and my feet from falling..'

---

[114] That is to say, a married woman. Unmarried mothers might, in earlier centuries, find that they were publicly reproached and made to do penance instead of welcomed back. The civil authorities might also administer punishment for her offence.

The appointed prayer also refers to 'the pain and peril of childbirth'. The woman's experience, with the possible fears and dangers that she had suffered, was fully acknowledged, and the Church welcomed her back, giving thanks for her safe delivery. Often the service was followed by communion; symbolically, and actually, she was out of her 'confinement'.

A service following childbirth was included in the Book of Common Prayer from the start, despite the reservations of many of the Protestant reformers. It was adapted from the old Latin Sarum rite, which in its turn has its origins in the Jewish rite of purification prescribed in Leviticus[115]. The 1549 Prayer Book called it 'The Order for the Purification of Women' but three years later in the 1552 Prayer Book this title was changed to the 'Thanksgiving of Women after Child-birth, commonly called the Churching of Women'. Originally the woman had knelt at or outside the church door, (1549 says the 'choir door') but the 1552 Prayer Book says that the woman should kneel in the chancel, near the altar. This change of place also emphasises the Protestant approach that this is not a superstitious rite of purification, but a thanksgiving[116].

---

[115] Chapter 12

[116] The Roman Catholic church kept not only the rite for the Blessing of a Woman after Childbirth, but also the Blessing of an Expectant Mother. Nowadays the Blessing after Childbirth may usually be incorporated into the Baptism service.
The rubric says that the woman should wait at the church door, kneeling and holding a lighted candle.

Popular superstition, which takes a long time to fade, despite the best efforts of the Church, continued to regard an 'unchurched' woman, and indeed, an unbaptised baby, as somehow unlucky. This suggests that the idea of 'pollution' by childbirth and 'purification' by the ceremony lingered long in the popular imagination[117]. Vicars working in the poorer parts of Sheffield in the 1980s, for instance, say that they still encountered this belief among their parishioners.

By the 1960s however, the practice of 'churching' had almost died out, partly because church going had declined. The pains and perils of childbirth had also reduced considerably, and many women, influenced more by the popular perception of the ceremony as purification, resented the suggestion that the sexual act of the conception, or that childbirth might have in some way rendered them unclean. Vicars, also, tended to dislike the overtones of superstition and so did not encourage their parishioners to ask for the service.

The Church of England Synod in the 1960s and 70s discussed the idea of replacing the Churching of Women service with a short service of Thanksgiving for the Birth (or Adoption) of a Child, and in 1974 Synod authorised three new services, which were included in the Alternative Service Book 1980: Thanksgiving for the Birth of a Child, Thanksgiving after Adoption and Prayers after the Birth of a still-born Child or the Death of

---

[117] Even the Puritan John Milton speaks of 'child-bed taint' in Sonnet XXIII, the one that begins: 'Methought I saw my late espoused saint…'. His wife died in 1658.

a newly-born Child. However, only the last of these three services contains a prayer that refers to the mother's experience of childbirth:

Loving Father, in your mercy you have brought your daughter N through childbirth in safety: We pray that she will know your support in this time of trouble and enjoy your protection always....[118]

The Thanksgiving for the Birth of a Child simply refers to *' a safe delivery and .. the privilege of parenthood'*[119]

These two thanksgiving services have now been merged into 'Thanksgiving for the Gift of a Child' in Common Worship. It is included in the section called Rites on the Way: Approaching Baptism. This is designed with a number of possibilities, to suit either birth or adoption, and does contain an optional prayer that can be used if there has been a 'difficult birth'

Loving Father, you have turned pain into joy by the birth of N [this child]. May N [this mother], remembering no longer her anguish, trust you in all things. As she asks for all she would receive[120]*, may she discover that in you her joy is complete; through Jesus your Son.*

While we can appreciate the motivation for dropping a service which was little used and smacked of folkloric superstition, it may be that we have failed to take account of the healing power of liturgy to express our deepest fears in a

---

[118] ASB 1980 p.322
[119] Ibid p.213
[120] Your authors are not sure what this phrase means. Will the mother understand?

way that relieves their hold on us. The terrors and pains of childbirth still exist, women still die as a result, and for some women it is no exaggeration to speak of the trauma of birth. The reason that superstitions persist is that they have a deep hold on our primitive selves. Rational argument cannot adequately counter these. The modern prayers that we have quoted seem inadequate in the face of this; they gloss over the birth experience and rather tritely suggest that the baby is a healing compensation for everything the mother (and father) has undergone. By contrast, the BCP service fully acknowledges what may have happened, and welcomes the woman back into her church. Properly used, or even combined with the prayers and ritual such as anointing that are used in healing ministry it may well assist with the healing and recovery process.

We think that there is a real place for it in the 'repertoire' of liturgical response, and ministers should be prepared to tell people that such prayers exist and offer them where appropriate. They may be more suited to a private service, at home, or in church quietly before a public service. In a modern context, the father or second parent should have the opportunity of being part of the rite; the experience of witnessing a birth can be traumatic for a partner as well, leaving them feeling helpless and hurt by what they have seen. We have attempted to draft a suitable service which is included at Appendix 1 on page179.

Thanksgiving for the Gift of a Child
Children used to be baptized very quickly after their births, within a week or so, as a general

rule[121]. In modern times, baptisms tend to be delayed, partly because parents want to organize a party as a celebration - not the easiest thing to do immediately after a birth. Also, the fear that an unbaptised child is somehow unlucky, or may be excluded from heaven if it dies, has faded from popular sensibility. So thanksgiving services are often used soon after the birth (or adoption) of the child as a form of welcome into the congregation. This was clearly how the compilers of ASB originally envisaged the service being used; that was the logic of its substitution for the Churching of Women.

The Methodist Service Book (1999) also included An Act of Thanksgiving after the Birth or Adoption of a Child[122], and makes the point that the service can be used as a welcome by the congregation where children have been adopted who have already been baptised. It is not suggested that it is used for every birth but observes that 'Prior to a child's baptism the parents *may have some particular reason for* [123] wishing to give thanks for his/her arrival.'
The service does not refer to the circumstances of the birth of the child at all; the child is described as a 'gift from God', as though a divine stork has deposited the child in the parents' arms.

---

[121] In the nineteenth century however, particularly in London, where parishes were populous and many people were not churchgoers, children in a single family were often baptised in a batch. This suggests that the superstitious power of baptism was waning.
[122] The 1975 book did not have such a service
[123] Our italics

The Anglican service has prayers of welcome and blessing to be said for a new baby, and delight expressed at his or her safe arrival. The mother's experience of the birth is, as we have seen, rather glossed over, but nevertheless the liturgy allows the church to express its welcome to the new arrival. It is often a service of great happiness, in which the small family unit can be enfolded in the larger church family.

However, over the last thirty years, it has changed in usage, and in many cases has become what can only be described as Baptism-lite. Common Worship recognizes this in the preface to the service which says:

It is designed to meet the needs of:
¶ parents who see this as a preliminary to Baptism;
¶ parents who do not wish their children to be baptized immediately;
¶ others, who do not ask for Baptism, but who recognize that something has happened for which they wish to give thanks to God.

The compilers of Common Worship plainly envisaged that this service could be used as a substitute for baptism. There is an optional point in the service at which the parents may be asked to name the child. 'Supporting friends' may also take part in the service and it is suggested that they may stand with the parents and say 'informal words.' These sections were not in the ASB service.

The result is that there is a lamentable confusion in what the service is intended for and how it is used. It is often used when a 'new' baby is several months, or even over a year old, thus losing much of its liturgical impact .

The 'gift' of a child
We have some reservations about the use of the term 'gift' for the arrival of a child into a family. Both the Anglican and the Methodist services use the word. We realise that it has been chosen as a term to embrace both birth and adoption, and to suggest that the child's arrival is a 'good thing', but it may not be the best metaphor to invoke.

In the Common Worship service the Minister asks the parents:
Do you receive these children as a gift from God?
To which they are expected to respond: *'We do'*.
It is a prescriptive question, suggesting that this is the only way of looking at the child's arrival. What, we wonder, would happen if the parents wanted to qualify their response? Is this a rather bullying use of liturgy: this is how you must think of your child? Though a child may feel to its parents like a gift, this is not always the case, and the metaphor rather implies that God may withhold children as much as bestow them on parents[124]. This is not a helpful idea for parents who have struggled to conceive a child, or who have not been able to conceive a child naturally. Does it feel a comfortable image for people who have undergone fertility treatment, or had a child through a surrogacy arrangement? It may do, but it may be insensitive to use it without discussion with the parents. The New Zealand Prayer Book

---

[124] Is this dangerously close to suggesting that the absence of children is punishment?

also uses the word 'gift', but, more subtly, implies that the child is given to the world. The minister, at the start of the service, says:
'we have come to celebrate the gift of this child
born into the world;
given to us
to love, to nurture, and to enjoy.'
This is, we suggest, a preferable emphasis.

However, there is another issue with the metaphor: 'gift' implies ownership. When a gift is made, the ownership of the gift passes from the giver to the receiver. The implication of this is that children are objects to be owned by their parents, not people in their own right. It might be preferable to refer to the wisdom of Kahlil Gibran, expressed in The Prophet:

Your children are not your children.
They are the sons and daughters of Life's longing for itself.
They come through you but not from you,
And though they are with you yet they belong not to you.

The danger of using language that implies ownership of children is that it reinforces something that many people do feel, but is not a healthy way of looking at family relationships. Family lawyers often have to deal with disputes about children in which parents, unhelpfully, treat their children and their children's time as quantifiable commodities, capable of being divided up with scant regard to their children's feelings or needs.

Contrast the Common Worship prayer that the parents say with the New Zealand Prayer Book:

Common Worship
God our creator, we thank you for the gift of these children, entrusted to our care. May we be patient and understanding, ready to guide and to forgive, so that through our love they may come to know your love; through Jesus Christ our Lord. Amen.
A New Zealand Prayer Book
God our creator, thank you for the waiting and the joy, thank you for new life and for parenthood, thank you for the gift of N, entrusted to our care. May we be patient and understanding, ready to guide and to forgive, that in our love N may know your love. May s/he learn to love your world and the whole family of your children; through Christ our life. Amen.

Both, to be sure, use the words 'gift' and 'entrusted to our care', but the NZ Prayer Book implies that the child is part of a wider community and the parents are taking the responsibility for him or her within that context.

When should the a Thanksgiving Service be used?

It might be preferable to be explicit about how the service is to be used and rename and restructure the service as a service of Welcome and Blessing for (A) New Child(ren) and for New Parents.

The intention would then clearly be that it could be used for:
- Members of a congregation who want to mark a birth or adoption soon after it has taken place so that a child can be formally welcomed into the church community
- Parents who feel that they want to offer formal thanks in church for a new arrival in a family, or a new assumption of a parental role.

In such a service there could also be a better emphasis on the parents, rather than the child. Often, such services are a sort of formal church cooing over the baby. The prayers that are included in the back of the Anglican service, for the parents, the home family, brothers and sisters, grandparents, should be remembered. They should also be rewritten and adapted to acknowledge the new family structures. For instance, the child may have a second (female) parent instead of a father, or have been carried by a surrogate mother; families may have adopted older children. The service could also be adapted to recognise the situation where a step-parent takes on Parental Responsibility for his or her step-children. This assumption of loving responsibility is surely something that calls for supportive prayer and blessing in whatever context.

Naming ceremonies

This then leaves the question of what to do about naming ceremonies. There is no doubt that people feel that there is a need for these. There has been a huge rise in the number of secular naming ceremonies, which suggests that this is a liturgy that people want. Councils now offer these ceremonies as part of the services offered by the local Register Office. Should the Church seek to meet this need in a way that is not baptism?

Christian faith and practice sets great store by names. We see ourselves as called, and called as individuals, by name.

Fear not, for I have redeemed you.
I have called you by name, you are mine.[125]

Christians acknowledge that names have significance. People may change their names at confirmation, or when they make their vows entering religious orders, choosing their new name to reflect their religious devotion. Parents generally spend a good deal of time considering names, choosing them not just for sound, or fashion, but with historical or family resonances. Just as when we launch a ship, we name it, the naming of a child is a way of helping it set out on his or her journey through the world, with a personal identity. It is fitting for the Church, whether the child is a regular part of the congregation or not, to greet this individual, as a child of God and pray for that journey.

There is scope here for a much more imaginative approach to a naming ceremony, in which the parents or godparents are asked to say the child's name, and if they wish, explain why it was chosen. Readings may be appropriate at this point, or an object or photograph of a person the child has been named after might be displayed.

A naming ceremony might be part of a Thanksgiving, or, if the child is baptized in the

---

[125] Isaiah 43.1

first few months of his/her life, part of that service. We will consider the use of naming in Baptism in the next section.

Baptism

Purists might take the view that a discussion of liturgy in the family context should not concern itself with Baptism, since this is properly a rite of initiation into the Christian faith. It is therefore *not* a naming ceremony, *nor* a celebration of a birth; instead, it marks the start of a Christian life in the Church. This is something that the Church has been at pains to point out ever since infant baptism became common practice, but it fights a losing conceptual battle; the approach of most families, even regular church goers, is that it is all three of these things. If the parents are not married, or civil partners, this may be their first opportunity to have their relationship affirmed, if only tangentially, in a formal ceremony of any kind. It is also therefore, in many communities, the excuse for a great party. Regular congregations can find themselves swamped by baptism families and friends, dressed to the nines and ill at ease with church customs and manners. It can sometimes be hard to exercise the hospitality and welcome that the Kingdom demands of us. In some parishes demand for baptism is so high that it cannot regularly take place at the main morning Sunday service[126], but instead baptisms take place at a separate service, and often in 'batches'.[127]

---

[126] which is where Common Worship plainly envisages as the ideal setting

[127] BCP gives us a historical perspective on this. It says that baptisms should normally take place after the last lesson at Morning or Evening prayer, with the regular congregation

Although Canon Law[128] says that a minister may not refuse to baptise a child in his or her parish, many ministers act as gatekeepers to this service. Baptism is sometimes refused (or so heavily discouraged that it feels to the parents as a refusal). Some ministers refuse baptism if parents are cohabiting, or same sex, or are not regular church goers. Many ministers feel it appropriate to stress that baptism requires a solemn commitment on the part of the parents and godparents. They may require parents to go through a course of baptism preparation or fulfil other conditions before the service can take place. We are concerned that the new family structures that we have outlined in this book may give some ministers further excuses for refusing or discouraging baptism. Many families find that the Thanksgiving service is offered instead, and they are not knowledgeable enough about liturgy and theology to understand the distinction that is being made[129]. Some are unaware that their child has not been baptised. The term 'christening', used loosely, seems to have aided this confusion.

Baptism, from an Anglican point of view, is a sacrament. Of the seven sacraments recognised by the Roman Catholic Church, Anglicans

---

present, and also clearly expects that there is likely to be more than one child at a time presented.

[128] B22, 5

[129] A priest told us about the baptism he had conducted for the second child of a family. The family had said that the elder child had been christened, but after the baptism he conducted, they commented that the priest at the first one hadn't used water.

retained two: communion and baptism[130]. A sacrament is, according to the Catechism, an outward and visible sign of an inward and spiritual grace. It is the public acknowledgement of our relationship with God, and of his love to us. The essential quality of grace is that it is undeserved; it is given to us freely, not because of our merits or actions. George Herbert, in his treatise on the life of a country parson says: 'baptism [is] a blessing that the world hath not the like.'[131]

What does baptism do?

Unfortunately, the position of the Church of England with regard to the effect of baptism is far from unanimous.

Here are a number of explanations about what Baptism is, arranged chronologically:

> ***1662 BCP Baptism service:*** *'..forasmuch as all men are conceived and born in sin, and that our Saviour Christ saith, none can enter into the kingdom of God, except he be regenerate and born anew of Water and the Holy Ghost..'*
>
> ***1662 BCP 39 Articles****: '....a sign of Regeneration or new Birth, whereby, as by an instrument[132], they that receive Baptism rightly are grafted into the Church; the promises of forgiveness of sin, and of*

---

[130] On the basis that these are the only two that Jesus performed in the Gospels

[131] *A Priest to His Temple*: from Chapter XXII 'The Parson in Sacraments'

[132] that is, a legal document. Note that the legal language continues in 'signed and sealed'.

our adoption to be the sons of God by the Holy Ghost, are visibly signed and sealed:…
1980 ASB: *'In the Gospel Jesus tells us that unless a man has been born again, he cannot see the Kingdom of God…God gives us a way to a second birth, a new creation and life in union with him…... Baptism is the sign and seal of this new birth'*
2000 Common Worship: *Baptism marks the beginning of a journey with God which continues for the rest of our lives, the first step in response to God's love.*
2011 Cof E website: *In baptism, parents thank God for his gift of life, make a decision to start the child on the journey of faith and ask for the Church's support.*

The uncertainty over what exactly baptism did was demonstrated by the Gorham case in the mid-nineteenth century.[133] Bishop Phillpotts of Exeter, a high churchman who believed that baptism brought about a change in the nature of a child, refused to institute the Reverend C.G. Gorham to a living in his diocese because the latter held that baptism marked a change of status, not a change of nature in a baptised child. The matter was referred ultimately to the Judicial Committee of the Privy Council, which concluded that Gorham's views were not at variance with the way in which the Anglican Articles of Religion had been interpreted by Anglican divines whose orthodoxy had never been questioned. However, the controversy revealed that there were widely differing views about baptism in the Church of

---

[133] See P.J .Jagger, *Clouded Witness. Initiation in the Church of England in the Mid-Victorian Period, 1850-1875*, Pennsylvania: Pickwick Publications, 1982, pp. 8-55.

England at the time. None of these issues were addressed in the important report of the Commission on Christian Doctrine, *Doctrine in the Church of England* (1938). Instead, baptism was defined as a rite which 'signifies and effects spiritual cleansing, "death unto sin and new birth unto righteousness" through incorporation into the Body of Christ, the Church'.[134] Most likely this formulation was the result of a compromise of the views of the members of the Commission, but it was not only an instance in which the piety of the language obscured the lack of the clarity of thought; it gave the unfortunate impression that baptism was primarily a rite of admission to the church.

The position that we hold has its origins in the Broad Church theologians of the nineteenth century and liberal catholic writers of the twentieth century, such as Oliver Quick. F.W. Robertson of Brighton, preaching in the immediate aftermath of the Gorham case, argued that baptism did not effect a change in a baptised child, but declared something to be the case.[135] '[B]aptism does not *create* a child of God. It authoritatively declares him so'. For Robertson, the fact that all children belong to God was something revealed by Jesus, and baptism was the means by which this revealed truth was publicly declared in the case of each child baptised. 'Baptism is a visible witness to the world of that

---

[134] *Doctrine in the Church of England. The Report of the Commission on Christian Doctrine Appointed by the Archbishops of Canterbury and York in 1922*, London: SPCK, 1938, p. 136.
[135] F. W. Robertson, *Sermons Preached at Brighton, Second Series*, London: Kegan Paul, Trench & Co., 1889, pp. 54-56.

which the world is for ever forgetting. A common Humanity united in God'. For the individual, baptism was a means of declaring that the baptised not only belonged to God, but was a member of Christ and an inheritor of the kingdom of heaven. To know and acknowledge these facts was to be regenerate. Baptism played a part in enabling people to come to know what was true in their case. An important implication of this view was that baptism included becoming a member of the church, but was much more than that. It was a public declaration of a truth about the nature of reality in general, and of an individual in particular.

In Quick's characteristically subtle and realistic discussion of baptism in *The Christian Sacraments* an element is emphasised that is underplayed in Robertson's exposition. For Quick, baptism is 'an extension and effect of the Incarnation and Atonement'.[136] If Jesus revealed the Fatherhood of God, he did it not by way of merely imparting information but by creating through the Incarnation and Atonement a new sphere of reality to which God wishes all to gain access. We can add that such a view fully accords with Paul's teaching about Adam and Christ as two spheres, the latter of which humans belong to by means of baptism and faith.[137] Quick is fully aware of the paradoxes implicit in the practice of baptism: that if only the declarative side is emphasised then nothing is effected 'beyond a vivid presentation of a universal truth', but that if

---

[136] O. C. Quick, *The Christian Sacraments*, London: Nisbet & Co., 1927, p. 161.
[137] Romans 5.12-6.11.

the sacrament is held to be the exclusive way of entering the new life then the Fatherhood of God ceases to be universal and 'is a relation which exists only towards the regenerate'.[138] The truth is obtained by holding both sides of the contradiction together.

Our view is that in the ministry, death and exaltation of Jesus, God has inaugurated a New Creation to which all may have access. Access is primarily, but not exclusively, by baptism accompanied by a confession of faith. In the case of infants, faith is expressed by others on behalf of the child, until the child is old enough to make a profession of faith. Although it is desirable that those responsible for the child should be believers, it is not indispensable that they should be so. What God has done for a child in Jesus Christ does not depend upon the faith or lack of it on the part of others. The church, in baptising infants, publicly declares what God has done in Christ, and pledges to the child the benefits that Christ's saving work have made available.

What do the promises require?
Why then, does it seem appropriate for ministers to hedge baptisms about with conditions that must be fulfilled by the parents and/or godparents? Part of the difficulty may be in the liturgy, and the changes from the ASB onwards.

BCP and its predecessors make it clear that the role of the godparents in the service is to respond as proxies for the child; the child is too young to answer the questions or make a

---

[138] Quick, *Sacraments*, p. 162.

profession of faith, so the godparents must answer on the child's behalf. Godparents are also 'sureties'. In legal terms a surety is the person who guarantees the payment of a debt. If the debtor does not pay, they are liable. The godparents are therefore taking on a responsibility to see that the child will in due course be able to make the promises and declaration of faith for him/herself. The natural assumption of BCP is that godparents will themselves be baptised and confirmed, versed in the faith and prepared to take their vows seriously, for fear of hell fire, if for no other motive. By the 20th century these assumptions could no longer be made.

ASB 1980 therefore changed the wording of the promises and profession of faith. Parents and godparents are addressed by the Priest:

> *Those who bring children to be baptized must affirm their allegiance to Christ and their rejection of all that is evil.*
> *It is your duty to bring up these children to fight against evil and to follow Christ.*
> *Therefore I ask these questions which you must answer <u>for yourselves and for these children.</u>*[139]
> *Do you turn to Christ?*
> **I turn to Christ.**
> *Do you repent of your sins?*
> **I repent of my sins.**
> *Do you renounce evil?*
> **I renounce evil.**

Further on in the service the parents and godparents are called on to make a profession of

---

[139] our emphasis

faith. Again, this is preceded with the instruction: 'you must answer *for yourselves and for these children'*. The congregation are asked to back this up by making their own declaration of faith.

Common Worship has reversed this approach, to some extent. Only adult candidates are asked to make a profession of faith for themselves. The whole congregation makes a profession of faith when a baby is baptised, and the parents and godparents are not singled out for a declaration. As to the promises, the parents and godparents answer *for* the child, according to the rubric:

At the baptism of children, the president then says to the parents and godparents

>……….*In baptism these children begin their journey in faith.*
>*<u>You speak for them today</u>[140].*
>*Will you care for them,*
>*and help them to take their place*
>*within the life and worship of Christ's Church?*
>**With the help of God, we will.**
>*The president addresses the candidates*
>*directly, <u>or through their</u> parents, godparents and sponsors*
>*In baptism, God calls us out of darkness into his marvellous light.*
>*To follow Christ means dying to sin and rising to new life with him.*
>*Therefore I ask:*
>*Do you reject the devil and all rebellion against God?*

---

[140] Our emphasis here and below

I reject them.
Do you renounce the deceit and corruption of evil?
I renounce them.
Do you repent of the sins that separate us from God and neighbour?
I repent of them.
Do you turn to Christ as Saviour?
I turn to Christ.
Do you submit to Christ as Lord?
I submit to Christ.
Do you come to Christ, the way, the truth and the life?
I come to Christ.

Unfortunately, in our view, the language has reverted to speak of the devil, and has become more wordy. The rubric does give the alternative of using the ASB promises, 'where there are strong pastoral reasons', though it is not explicit what these might be. Are elegance of expression and pith strong pastoral reasons?

The ASB changes required a more explicitly serious and committed approach to Baptism than had obtained previously. It certainly gave ministers a basis for requiring evidence of Christian belief and practice in the parents and godparents before a Baptism could go ahead. The Common Worship service has been criticised for not demanding this, for, as it were, relaxing the rules.

Plainly we have moved a long way from the belief that an unbaptised baby is mired in original sin and therefore shut out of heaven. The Protestant view of Baptism at the Reformation was that the Roman rite contained far too much that smacked of magic and superstition. The child was exorcised at the church door – the evil one was conjured out of him or her, and salt, out of which the devil had also been exorcised was placed on the child's tongue[141]. Only then was the child brought into the church. The first Prayer Book of Edward also contained an exorcism[142], but this was dropped by the second Prayer Book. However BCP and even ASB plainly declare that Baptism does something to the child, that it makes a difference, that it gains the child entry to the Kingdom of God. ASB ducks the question about what happens to you if you haven't got this pass code. Common Worship (and it has been criticised for this) moves a long way from this. Mindful that the sacraments are expressions of undeserved grace, we welcome this less minatory and inclusive approach.

What do parents seek for their children?

So, we return to the question of why people seek baptism for their babies. The simple answer,

---

[141] The modern Roman Catholic rite still includes an exorcism, though in rather toned down language.
[142] 'I commaude thee, uncleane spirite, in the name of the father, of the sonne, and of the holy ghost, that thou come out, and departe from these infantes, whom our Lord Jesus vouchsaued, to call to his holy Baptisme, to be made members of his body , and of his holy congregacion. Therfore thou cursed spirite,remember thy sentence, remember thy judgemente, remember the daye to be at hande, wherin though shalte borne in fyre euerlasting, prepared for the and thy Angels. And presume not hereafter to exercise any tyranne towarde these infants, whom Christe hathe bought with his precious bloud, and by this his holy Baptisme calleth to be of his flocke.

which will not please some church people, is because it is the custom: it is the traditional response to a birth. It is the done thing. It has religious significance to those who have a religious approach to life. It is also significant in a customary or even superstitious way. One is reminded of Lady Bracknell's response to Jack Worthington when he asks if he had been christened before he was left in the infamous handbag: 'Every luxury that money could buy, including christening, had been lavished on you by your fond and doting parents.'[143] We should also ask why baptism is still offered and sought for the sickly newborn child. There is something powerful and primitive going on in our minds and feelings. It is possible to see this as a ceremony which adult parents need more than their babies. It marks a child as an individual, important soul, a distinct person. It confirms that God recognizes the child just as much as its parents. Now, to those of strong faith, this might never have been in doubt. But not all of us are, and the more reassurance that the ceremonies of faith can impart, the better.

Naming in the Baptism Service

Baptism is also, in most people's eyes, a naming ceremony, as the term "Christian name" suggests. Legally it retains this function. A name given at baptism may be substituted on the birth certificate if it is confirmed by the minister who has charge of the baptismal register. Civil naming ceremonies do not have this legal significance.

---

[143] Act III, *The Importance of Being Earnest*, Oscar Wilde

The Anglican Church obviously wants to steer people away from this approach. The mind-set of the 16th century Protestant reformers is still there. People need to be taken away from their benighted superstitions. Though the BCP service firmly asks the godparents to 'Name this child', this part of the rite (which for many people is very significant) has been removed. In the ASB and Common Worship services there is no opportunity to name the child formally, though its name will be used as it is baptized. As we have argued, names are significant to us. Why should we not name a child (or an adult) at baptism, reinforcing their new identity and new birth?

Parenting in the Baptism Service
There is only one prayer in the Common Worship service for the parents, who are described rather coolly as carers. This may be out of a spirit of inclusivity, but seems a little impersonal:

Faithful and loving God,
bless those who care for these children
and grant them your gifts of love, wisdom and faith.
Pour upon them your healing and reconciling love,
and protect their home from all evil.
Fill them with the light of your presence
and establish them in the joy of your kingdom,
through Jesus Christ our Lord.

The service has been criticized not only for its inaccessible language but also its omission to speak, except in passing, of how love underpins the whole of our relationship with God and with other people. Contrast with that the Minister's address to the candidates in the Methodist service[144]:

> N and N
> for you Jesus Christ came into the world;
> for you he lived and showed God's love;
> for you he suffered death on the Cross;
> for you he triumphed over death,
> rising to newness of life;
> for you he prays at God's right hand
> all this for you
> before you could know anything of it.
> In your Baptism
> the word of Scripture is fulfilled:
> 'We love, because God first loved us.'

The Common Worship Baptism service demands very little of parents and god-parents in terms of precise theological adherence or practice. There is a simple promise at the beginning:

> *Parents and godparents, the Church receives these children with joy.*
> *Today we are trusting God for their growth in faith.*
> *Will you pray for them,*
> *draw them by your example into the community of faith*
> *and walk with them in the way of Christ?*
> **With the help of God, we will.**

There should not therefore, in theory, be grounds for refusing to baptise a child on the basis of its parents' lifestyle, sexual orientation, or family structure. We do not mean to suggest that this means that Baptism should not be taken seriously. Ministers still have a pastoral responsibility to teach those who seek it what it

---

[144] Methodist Worship Book 1999

means and the expectations of the Church. But it is not a good conduct prize, to be awarded to a child on the basis of its family's merit.

Churches also need to be aware that the standard form of Baptism register needs amendment to accommodate second parents and other family arrangements.

A three or four-fold service?
We have considered the various rites that may be appropriate after a birth, or adoption, or taking on of Parental Responsibility. They are:
- Prayers of thanks and healing after a birth
- Thanksgiving for a child
- Naming of a child
- Baptism

We suggest that a Thanksgiving service should have a flexible liturgy so that it can be used appropriately to welcome a very newborn child, or one who may be several months old.

We can envisage all four of these services being used in suitable combinations to meet the needs of families. Some might want the first three all together soon after a birth, and then have a Baptism later. Others, coming to a church at a later interval, might feel that at this stage they want Thanksgiving and Naming. The possibility of a later Baptism remains. Or people who have come to the minister in a more conventional way some months after a birth simply asking for a christening, might feel that Baptism, or Naming and Baptism might be what they seek. As we have indicated, we feel that the Baptism Service should include naming explicitly.

Ministers should be clear about the options and what the implications of each are, but not suggest that any family's child is unworthy of Baptism because of his or her parents' relationship or sexuality. To do so is to negate the gospel message and the nature of the sacrament: that it represents to us undeserved grace.

Other liturgies for parents and families
One of the things that struck us when we first discussed the ideas for this book was how parenting has been taken for granted by the church for so long. The modern media are full, it seems, of comments on and advice to, parents. Nowadays parenting is regarded as a skill, something that can be learned and improved upon. We do not take it for granted that someone who produces a baby will automatically know how to look after it and bring it up, bolstered by the example of previous generations and the extended family. We acknowledge that what happens to a child in the very earliest part of its life has a very significant effect on its psychological and emotional wellbeing. Good parenting is not necessarily instinctive, and is not easy. It calls for exercise of all the 'Christian virtues' plus a sense of humour[145] and sense of proportion.

Traditionally the attitude of the Church seems to have been that being a parent is natural, so get on with it. Parents are exhorted to bring their children up in the faith and set a Christian example, but there isn't very much in our liturgy

---

[145] which isn't a classic 'Christian virtue' but really ought to be

that prays for parents themselves, acknowledges that it can be difficult, and offers encouragement and support. This may be because of the ambiguity towards marriage that the Church had historically displayed, which we have discussed earlier. If you really must marry and procreate, the Church seems to be saying, then you are on your own.

The only occasion on which the Church seems to address the question of parenthood is on Mothering Sunday, the fourth Sunday in Lent[146]. This has its name from the custom of congregations returning to the mother church on the 4th Sunday in Lent to celebrate Laetare Sunday, a relatively cheerful celebration to lighten the gloom of fasting Lent. It is said that the early church incorporated the Roman festival of the mother goddess Cybele, which fell in March, and gave it a new Christian gloss, focusing on the Virgin Mary. Since the 1920s in Britain churches have conflated the festival with a celebration of motherhood in general[147], and, in recent years, there has been an explosion of commercial exploitation for the Sunday.

The result, liturgically, has been a tendency to rather mawkish and sentimental services extolling the traditional virtues of womanly motherhood. Posies are often provided by the church for children to give to their mothers.

---

[146] This is popularly called Mothers' Day, thus confusing it with Mother's Day in America, a festival that has nothing to do with the Church, and which falls on the second Sunday in May

[147] inspired by the American institution of Mother's Day

Modern feminists may find much of this hard to take. Women who have not had children, especially if they long for them, may find such services unbearable. So may people who are mourning the death of their mothers. Fathers may feel that their role as parents is being completely ignored, and feel devalued. These services tend to be a long way away from what being a parent is really like.

The Church of England, in an attempt to redress the gender balance, has published[148] a service that can be used for Father's Day [149], which is another secular festival much beloved of card manufacturers, and not a feast of the Church at all. The service draws heavily on the metaphor of God the Father, and also includes (though this, like all the service is published as suggestions rather than official liturgy) a recital of the Ten Commandments. There is only one prayer for fathers themselves, in which, inevitably, the example of Joseph is invoked. Given that Joseph is a step, or adoptive father to Jesus, and Mary's pregnancy might be seen as an example of surrogacy, using Joseph as the paradigm of fatherhood here might be seen as boldly inclusive. However, we fear that this actually invokes the 'holy family' cliché that we discussed in Chapter 5. There are other biblical fathers, though not all enjoy the best of relationships with their children. David, after all, was very loving towards his children, though perhaps he would be felt to be too indulgent to be invoked in prayer as an example. And, his matrimonial record is perhaps

---

[148] in New Patterns for Worship (2002)
[149] on the 3rd Sunday in June

not as respectable as conventional morality might hope for.

If the Church is going to show itself as taking parenthood seriously, there is a need for prayers and liturgies that recognise the joys and the difficulties of the experience, and do their best to support and encourage parents. Parents need spiritual food, not clichés which make them feel inadequate. If 'good enough' parenting[150] is a good thing, then this needs affirmation and celebration. Our faith should teach us that while we may never attain perfection in this life, we should realise that God loves us for who we are and as we are, not in spite of who we are. We bring our whole selves to God, not the edited highlights. We need to be careful that liturgy does not act as a deadening reproach for our failings. Instead, it should give us hope and inspiration.

We considered whether there was some other occasion on which the Church could celebrate the role of parents, all parents. The only saints in the Anglican list of saints' days as set out in Common Worship who are celebrated as a couple, and for their parental role, are saints Anne and Joachim, the parents of the Virgin Mary[151], whose feast day is 26th July, just about the time that schools traditionally break up for the summer holidays. Three days later on 29th July, we celebrate Mary, Martha and Lazarus, siblings who

---

[150] The expression comes from the influential work of Donald Winnicott and Bruno Bettelheim

[151] The only other married couple are William and Catherine Booth, the founders of the Salvation Army

appear to all live together in Bethany[152]. This seems a good time of year to have such a celebration. People who take on a parental role (whether related to the children or not) perform a 'mighty act of love'. Churches should be affirming this.

Marriage and Services of Prayer and Dedication
We have already described in Chapter 3 the legal position of a marriage, a civil marriage and a civil partnership. The law has recently been changed[153] so that a civil partnership may be celebrated in a place of worship, though this does not mean that a church can be compelled to allow this to take place. The Church of England has said that its churches may not do this for the time being without the sanction of General Synod.

If, and we hope, when, it does become possible for a partnership to be celebrated as a marriage, churches need to do some serious thinking about the images and scriptural references that they use, and the images that they convey. We are so used to some tropes that we do not pause to consider their implications. For instance,
they shall be united with one another in heart, body and mind,
as Christ is united with his bride, the Church[154].
implies (whether we like it or not, as we have observed) that Christ has sex with his Church. This is a very ancient metaphor, which the Church has lived and worked with since the time of St

---
[152] John Ch.11
[153] 11th December 2011
[154] Common Worship 2000

Paul[155]. The sexual relationship in this context is an unequal one: the bride is subservient to her husband, passive to his active sexual role. You can see that this is so, distasteful as the metaphor may be when put like that, if you consider whether you can continue to think of that image in the context of a same-sex couple. Depending on your sexual orientation this may make the metaphor better or worse in your mind. But it calls into question whether any of us feel comfortable in a modern age, with an image of marriage, used in a religious context, which necessarily assumes the dominance of one partner by the other, not only legally, but physically.

The 'giving away' of the bride reinforces the view of marriage as an unequal relationship: handed as a chattel from her father to her husband. There is undoubtedly something charming in the loving care a father can display in supporting his daughter on her important day, and many a nervous bride has clung to her father's arm for support as she wobbled down the church on unfamiliar heels. However it is good to see that Common Worship now includes this part of the service only as an optional extra, and instead of asking 'Who giveth this woman…' the minister now asks 'Who brings this woman to be married to this man?' which is marginally preferable. This still suggests that there is a transition from one family to another, but why is it only the bride who makes this transition? Same-sex relationships can highlight for us the inbuilt metaphors that have prevailed for so long. Would it not be better to imply by words and actions that

---

[155] 2 Corinthians, Ch 11 v 2, Ephesians, Ch 5, v 21 onward

both partners are leaving their families to form a new family?

One might also question the rather glib statement: *Marriage is a gift of God in creation*. The legal institutions we read about in the Old and New Testament are so far from our own circumstances that they can hardly be described with the same word. Adam and Eve, so often cited as the natural order of things, do not appear to have gone through any formal ceremony at all. What we do find, however, is that God is on the side, so to speak, of stable relationships of love, forbearance and kindness, that allow people to flourish together; households where children and other vulnerable people are looked after; relationships that are not based on a notion of ownership or unequal power. A sexual bond, which is where each person is at their most vulnerable and trusting with each other, builds that mutual love and togetherness. A loving relationship like this has a ripple effect, touching all others it comes in contact with. With those principles in mind it is surely possible to say that God blesses loving commitments of couples who intend and hope to spend their lives together in partnership.

If we think carefully about the metaphorical language that we use in these liturgies we may be able to craft prayers that recognize and invoke the beauty of a relationship of two different individuals who come together as equals to make an even better whole, the existence of which is not only a blessing for them but also for their families and the wider world. Happy and loving families are in their own way examples of the kingdom of heaven.

Services of Prayer and Dedication after a Civil Marriage
These are often referred to colloquially as services of Blessing, though that is precisely what they are not. They will generally be used where one, or both of a couple, have been divorced and their former spouse is still alive. It was this service that was held after the civil marriage of the Prince of Wales and the Duchess of Cornwall. The media inaccurately referred to this as a service of blessing. The Revd Brian Lewis, in a persuasively argued paper[156] suggests that a similar service (since it isn't a blessing) could, within Canon Law as it stands, be offered to a same-sex couple following their civil partnership.

The arguments about whether people who have been divorced should be allowed to remarry in church are too long to rehearse in the scope of this book but it seems to us that in its present attitude the Church of England is in danger of privileging divorce above all other 'sins'. How does such an attitude sit with doctrines of repentance and forgiveness? Further, do not all couples who propose to marry need all the emotional and spiritual help and support that they can get? The implication of only being allowed to have a service of Prayer and Dedication in such circumstances, is that this couple is somehow not worthy of grace, and the Church takes it upon itself to be the judge of that worthiness. It is similar to the gate-keeping attitude that says that

---

[156] http://inclusive-church.org.uk/about/church-services-after-civil-partnerships

some children are deserving of Baptism because of their family circumstances, others must make do with Thanksgiving.

Conclusion
Families and couples come to the Church asking for their commitment and love for each other and their children to be publicly recognized and supported in prayer. They should be met with love and hospitality. Our church structures and liturgies need to be designed to support and encourage stable, loving relationships that enable people to be cherished and flourish. Though unusual situations may require tailor-made responses, we should already be alert to the great variety of legitimate family structures. We should already have places set at the table to welcome the unexpected guests.

Bibliography

Lord Scarman, in <u>Gillick v West Norfolk and Wisbech Area Health Authority and Another</u> [1986], 1 FLR 224, HL

Abrahams, R. G., 1973, 'Some Aspects of Levirate' in J. Goody (ed.), *The Character of Kinship*, Cambridge: Cambridge University Press, pp. 163-174.

Barrett, C.K., 1968, *The First Epistle to the Corinthians* (Black's New Testament Commentaries), London: Adam & Charles Black.

Barth, K., 1957, *Kirchliche Dogmatik,* Bd.III *Die Lehre von der Schöpfung,* Vierter Teil, Zollikon-Zürich: Evangelischer Verlag.

Barton, S. C. (ed.), 1996, *The Family in Theological Perspective*, Edinburgh: T & T. Clark.

R. Baxter, R., 2000. *The Practical Works of Richard Baxter. 1 A Christian Directory,* Morgan, PA: Soli Deo Gloria Publications.

Beattie, J., 1964, *Other Cultures: Aims, Methods and Achievements in Social Anthropology,* London : Routledge & Kegan Paul.

Bede, 1962, *Historical Works* I, (Loeb Classical Library 246) Cambridge, Mass: Harvard University Press; London: Heinemann.

Beesley, P., 2010 3rd ed., *Anglican Marriage in England and Wales. A Guide to the Law for Clergy.* London: Faculty Office of the Archbishop of Canterbury.

Bell, G.K.A., 1952, 3rd ed., *Randall Davidson, Archbishop of Canterbury,* London: Oxford University Press.

J. Bergman 'Askese I', in *Theologische Realenzyklopädie* vol.4, Berlin: de Gruyter, pp.195-225.

Bettelheim,B., 1987 *A Good-Enough Parent: A Book on Child-Rearing,* NewYork: Knopf

Boecker, H. J., 1974 'Anmerkungen zur Adoption im Alten Testament', *Zeitschrift für die alttestamentliche Wissenschaft,* 86 pp. 86-8

Brink, L., 'Ehe/Eherecht/Ehescheidung VI' in *Theologische Realenzyklopädie,* Berlin: de Gruyter, vol 9, pp.330-332.

Burgière, A., et al (eds.), 1996, *Geschichte der Familie* vol 1, Darmstadt: Wissenschaftliche Buchgesellschaft. French original *Histoire de la famille,* Paris: Armand Colin 1986.

Clarke, W.K.L., 1932, 'Confirmation' in W.K.L.Clarke (ed.) *Liturgy and Worship. A Companion to the Prayer Books of the Anglican Communion.* London: SPCK.

Committee of the Royal Anthropological Institute of Great Britain and Ireland, 1954, 6th ed., *Notes and Queries in Anthropology,* London: Routledge and Kegan Paul

Cornish, F. W., 1910, *A History of the English Church in the Nineteenth Century,* Part II, London: Macmillan & Co.

Countryman, L. William, 2001 (new ed.), *Dirt, Sex and Greed,* London: SCM Press.

Cronzel, H., Ehe/Eherecht/Ehescheidung V' in *Theologische Realenzyklopädie* , Berlin: de Gruyter, vol 9, pp.325-327.

Danby, H., 1933, *The Mishnah,* Oxford: Oxford University Press.

Doctrine in the Church of England. The Report of the Commission on Christian Doctrine Appointed by the Archbishops of Canterbury and York in 1922, London: SPCK, 1938.

Dunn, J.D.G. 1996, 'The Household Rules in the New Testament' in S. C. Barton, (ed.),*The Family in Theological Perspective,* Edinburgh: T & T. Clark.

Gibran, Kahlil, 1923, *The Prophet,* New York: Knopf

Goody, J, (ed.), 1973, *The Character of Kinship,* Cambridge: Cambridge University Press.

Goody, J, 1983, *The Development of the Family and Marriage in Europe*, Cambridge: Cambridge University Press.

Green, M., 1980, 'Homosexuality and the Christian' in M. Green, D.Holloway, D.Watson, *The Church and Homosexuality. A Positive Answer to the Current Debate,* London: Hodder and Stoughton.

J.Gribomont 'Askese IV' in *Theologische Realenzyklopädie*, Berlin: de Gruyter vol.4

Harrison, C., 1996, 'The Silent Majority: the Family in Patristic Thought' in S. C. Barton (ed.) *The Family in Theological Perspective,* Edinburgh: T & T. Clark, pp.88-91.

Herbert, G., *A Priest to His Temple*: from Chapter XXII 'The Parson in Sacraments', *The English Poems of George Herbert with A Priest to the Temple and his collection of proverbs called Jacula Prudentium*, London and Sydney: Griffith Farran Okeden and Walsh

Honecker, M., 1995, *Grundriß der Sozialethik*, Berlin: de Gruyter.

Jagger, P. J., 1982, *Clouded Witness. Initiation in the Church of England in the Mid-Victorian Period, 1850-1875*, Pennsylvania: Pickwick Publications.

James, M. R., 1924, *The Apocryphal New Testament,* Oxford: Clarendon Press.

Knobloch, F.W. , Adoption' in *Anchor Bible Dictionary* vol. 1, pp.76-79

Luther, M., 1962, *Luther's Works,* vol.45, Philadelphia: Muhlenberg Press.

J. Maier 'Askese III' in *Theologische Realenzyklopädie,* Berlin: de Gruyter, vol.4,

L. Markert, 'Askese II' in *Theologische Realenzyklopädie*, Berlin: de Gruyter, vol.4,

Milton, J. Sonnet 'On His Blindness', in *The Oxford Book of English Verse*, 1939, Oxford: Oxford University Press

The Archbishops' Council, 2002, *New Patterns for Worship*, London: Church House Publishing

Otto, E, 1994, *Theologische Ethik des Alten Testaments*, Stuttgart: Kohlhammer Verlag.

Poole, Matthew, 1962, *A Commentary on the Holy Bible* (1685), Edinburgh: The Banner of Truth Trust.

Procter, F., W.H. Frere, 1905, 3rd ed., *A New History of The Book of Common Prayer. With a Rationale of its Offices*, London: Macmillan.

Quick, O. C., 1927, *The Christian Sacraments*, London: Nisbet & Co.

Robertson, F. W., 1898, *Sermons Preached at Brighton, Second Series*, London: Kegan Paul; Trench & Co.

Rogerson, J.W., 1978, *Anthropology and the Old Testament*, Oxford: Blackwell.

Rogerson, J., P.Davies, 2005 2nd ed. *The Old Testament World*, London: T. and T.Clark International.

Rogerson, J. W., 2007, *According to the Scriptures? The Challenge of Using the Bible in Social, Moral and Political Questions*, London: Equinox.

Rousselle, A., 1996, 'Die Familie im Römischen Reich: Zeichen und Gebärden' in A. Burgière et al (eds.) *Geschichte der Familie* vol 1, Darmstadt: Wissenschaftliche Buchgesellschaft. French original *Histoire de la famille*, Paris: Armand Colin 1986.

Stevenson, J, 1957, *A New Eusebius. Documents illustrative of the history of the church to AD 337*, London: SPCK.

Strack, H. L., P. Billerbeck, 1926, *Kommentar zum Neuen Testament aus Talmud und Midrasch*, vol. 1, Munich: C.H.Beck, 1926.

Stone, L., 1992, *Road to Divorce: England 1530 -1987* Oxford: Oxford University Press

Thane, P., 2011, *Happy Families,* British Academy Policy Centre: London www.britac.ac.uk/policy/Happy-families.cfm

Wilde, Oscar, Act III, *'The Importance of Being Earnest'*, from *Plays: Oscar Wilde,* Harmondsworth: Penguin

Winnicott, D. W., 1973, *The Child, the Family, and the Outside World* Harmondsworth: Penguin

Woodforde, James *The Diary of a Country Parson 1758 -1802* ed. James Beresford, 1999, Canterbury Press

Appendix 1

A service for a woman who has given birth [and the child's other parent]

This service is designed to take place quietly before the main Sunday service, at which the mother (and the other parent) together with the new baby will be welcomed back by the congregation. It could be said in a side chapel or quiet area of the church. It could also be used at home.

This service can be said by the mother and the minister alone, but if there is another parent who wishes to be present, we have written the service with him or her in mind, and the parent[s] may wish to invite other close friends to be there with them. We suggest that if the mother has no other supporter, a Reader, or other lay minister, or suitable chosen person from the church should be present to support her.

Minister	*N(mother)* [and *O (other parent)*] we have met today to thank God that you have come safely through childbirth and to welcome you back into the worshipping family of the Church. God our father and mother, you bring new life to birth every moment in your great work of creation with the tenderness of a parent, we thank you for *N's* safe delivery. We ask that the pains and fears that she has experienced

| | may fade in her memory
and not trouble her
and she may find new life and hope in you. |
| --- | --- |
| All | **Amen** |
| Minister | For generations women have come to church after child-birth and said this psalm, which reminds us that God is with us through pain and fear and even the danger of death, and gives thanks for safe deliverance.
So, in the company of all the mothers who have gone before you, and holding before God your own experience, we say: |
| *This may be said together or antiphon-ally, or used as a reading by the Minister* | 1 I love the Lord,
for he has heard the voice of my supplication;
because he inclined his ear to me
on the day I called to him.
2 The snares of death encompassed me;
the pains of hell took hold of me;
by grief and sorrow was I held.
3 Then I called upon the name of the Lord:
'O Lord, I beg you, deliver my soul.'
4 Gracious is the Lord and righteous;
our God is full of compassion.
5 The Lord watches over the simple;
I was brought very low and he saved me.
6 Turn again to your rest, O my soul,
for the Lord has been gracious to you.
7 For you have delivered my soul from death, |

	my eyes from tears and my feet from falling. 8 **I will walk before the Lord in the land of the living**. *Ps 116:1-8*
All	**Glory to God, Source of all being, Eternal Word and Holy Spirit; as it was in the beginning is now and shall be for ever. Amen**
	N [and O] may be anointed
Minister	*N [and O]* I anoint you in the name of God who gives you life and wholeness. Receive Christ's healing and love, and all the riches of his grace and peace.
All	**Amen**
Minister	God our father and mother we ask your blessing on *N* [and *O*] as *she/they sets/set* out to follow your mighty act of love in parenthood. Grant *her/them* patience and wisdom, humour and gentleness as *she/they* care[s] for ………….. May they grow in love and goodness to each other and, when their earthly lives have run their course be united with the whole family of your children in heaven.
All	**Amen**
Minister	May the Lord bless you and keep you. May the Lord make his face shine upon you

	and be gracious unto you.
	May the Lord lift up the light of his countenance upon you, and give you peace.
	And the blessing of the threefold God be upon you,
	and all whom you love,
	now, and evermore.
All	**Amen**

Answers
to Discussion Exercise at the end of Chapter 4

Abraham and Sarah — Genesis

Surrogacy arrangement	Sarah and Hagar Ch 16.
Childlessness	Sarah Ch 16 -17
Second marriage	Ch 25.1 Abraham married Keturah
Step-brothers	Ch 25.2. Isaac has 6 step-brothers
Concubines	Ch 25.6
Marriage breakdown	Look closely at Ch 22.19 and Ch 23.1. It looks as if following the attempted sacrifice of Isaac, Sarah never lived with Abraham again.
Long marriage	Sarah and Abraham She was 65 when they left Haran when Abraham was 75 - Ch12.4 (we know she is 10 years younger than Abraham – Ch 17.17) and dies at the age of 127 Ch 23.
Child sacrifice	Ch 12. Abraham prepared to do it

Jacob's family — Genesis

Polygamy	Jacob married Leah and Rachel Ch 29
Childlessness	Rachel is childless for many years Ch 29.31
Surrogacy arrangement	Both Rachel and Leah's maids bore children for their mistresses Ch 30. 1-13
Sibling rivalry	Jacob and Esau, and then

	Jacob's sons towards Joseph
Sex with sister-in-law	Onan and Tamar Ch 38.8-9
Sex with daughter-in-law	Judah with Tamar Ch 38.13-26
Concubines	Bilhah and Zilpah Ch 30
Death in childbirth	Rachel giving birth to Benjamin Ch 35.18

David	**2 Samuel**
Passionate same-sex relationship	However you view David and Jonathan's relationship, it was passionate in the sense of being very strongly and deeply felt. 2S Ch 1.26
Polygamy	David had many wives. I Chronicles.3 lists seven, omitting Michal, daughter of Saul, who was childless
Adultery	David with Bathsheba 2S Ch 11
Grieving over baby death	2S Ch 12. (and the mourning over Absalom)
Family rebellion	Absalom Ch 15 (and previously)
Concubines	Plenty – see Ch 5.13
Adopts lover's child	David adopted Jonathan's lame son Mephibosheth 1S Ch 9
Sibling rivalry	2S Ch 13. Absalom and Amnon

Moses	Exodus
Foreign marriage	Moses is recorded as having two wives, Zipporah and a Cushite woman Numbers Ch 12.1. Judges 1.16 also indicates there may have been a Kenite wife as well
Child mutilation	Zipporah, in an odd part of the story, circumcises their child to protect Moses Ch 4.25
Adoption	The Egyptian princess adopts Moses Ch 2.10

Index
Biblical references index
OLD TESTAMENT

Genesis 12.1-2; 26.6-16	114-115
Genesis 15.2-3	60
Genesis 16.1-4	57
Genesis 16.1-6	103
Genesis 19.15	56
Genesis 2.23-4	114
Genesis 2.23-4	99
Genesis 2.24	54, 100, 117, 122, 123
Genesis 22.1-10	63
Genesis 24	56
Genesis 24.15	102
Genesis 26.34, 38.9	55
Genesis 27.1-40	68
Genesis 27.5-29	113
Genesis 29	113
Genesis 29.13-30	102
Genesis 29.15-30	55
Genesis 30.1-8	57
Genesis 30.9-11	57-58
Genesis 31	113
Genesis 38	58-59
Genesis 48.5	60
Genesis 7.7	56
Exodus 2.10	60, 62
Exodus 2.21	55
Exodus 21.1-6	67
Exodus 21.7	63
Leviticus 18	102
Leviticus 18	111
Leviticus 18	99-100
Leviticus 18, 20	102
Leviticus 18.16	100
Leviticus 18.7-18	56

Leviticus 20.10   110-111
Leviticus 25   64
Numbers 12.1   55
Numbers 30.3-5   112
Numbers 30.6-15   112
Numbers 35.25   63
Deuteronomy 15.12-18   67, 125-126
Deuteronomy 15.14   62
Deuteronomy 15.2-3, 7-11, 12-18   64
Deuteronomy 16.11   62-63
Deuteronomy 21.15-17   56
Deuteronomy 21.18-21   63, 68
Deuteronomy 22.23-28   61
Deuteronomy 24.1   61
Deuteronomy 25   58
Deuteronomy 25.5-10   58, 59
Deuteronomy 6.6-7   110
Joshua 24.15   110
Judges 10.3-4   56
Judges 10.4   55
Judges 12.4   55
Judges 8.30   55
Ruth 1.16-17   114
Ruth 4.16   60
Ruth 4.17   59
1 Samuel 1.1-8   114
1 Samuel 1.2   55
1 Samuel 18.1-5   114
1 Samuel 2.19   68
1 Samuel 20.18-42   114
1 Samuel 3.13   110-111
1 Samuel 9.1   63-64
2 Samuel 12.1-5   69
2 Samuel 13   63, 113
2 Samuel 13.37-9   68
2 Samuel 18.33   68
2 Samuel 20.3   56

2 Samuel 9.1-8	64, 114
1 Kings 11.3	56
2 Kings 10.1	56
1 Chronicles 3.1-9	55
Nehemiah 5.5	63, 68
Esther 2.7; 15	59
Psalm 103.13	69
Psalm 116	137-138
Psalm 2.7	60
Psalm 22.9	69
Proverbs 13.24	69
Proverbs 2.1- 7.21	69
Ecclesiastes 4.9-12	110
Isaiah 40-55	69
Isaiah 43.1	148
Jeremiah 16.2	115
Ezekiel 16.4	63
Ezekiel 16.4-5	68

NEW TESTAMENT

Matthew 1.18-25	61
Matthew 1.25	61
Matthew 10.37	97
Matthew 19.21	97
Matthew 19.21, 29	100-101
Matthew 19.3-12	84
Matthew 19.4-5	99
Matthew 22	83-84
Matthew 22.23-33	103
Matthew 22.30	99
Mark 10.1-2	50
Mark 10.2-12	84
Mark 10.6-9	54
Mark 10.6-9	60-61
Mark 10.7	122
Mark 3	65
Mark 3.21	65

Mark 3.33-35	96-97
Mark 3.33-5	65
Luke 14.26	97
Luke 8.1-3	65
John 11	168
John 19.26	65-66
Acts 16.14-15, 33-34; 18.8	110
Acts 18.1-3	65
Acts 20.4-5	65
Acts 4.32-6	65
Romans 16.1-16	98
1 Corinthians 7.1	97
1 Corinthians 7.7-8, 32-35	110
1 Corinthians 7.8-10	48
1 Corinthians 7.8-9	97
1 Corinthians 7.32-34	99
1 Corinthians 9.19-23	127
2 Corinthians 11.2	169
2 Corinthians 3.6	123
Galatians 5.23	70
Ephesians 5.21	169
Ephesians 5.22- 6.9	66
Ephesians 5.22	96
Ephesians 5.22-3	99
Ephesians 5.22-33	49
Ephesians 5.25	49
Ephesians 5.31	117
Ephesians 5.32	117
Ephesians 51.19-20	67
Colossians 3.15- 4.1	66
Colossians 3.22-4	66
Colossians 4.16-17	67
Colossians 4.18	96
1 Thessalonians 4.13-5.11	98
1 Timothy 2.8-15; 6.1-2	66
1 Timothy 3.1-12	67
1 Timothy 3.2	61-62

Titus 2.1-10 — 66
Hebrews 19.1 — 68
1 Peter 2.18- 3.7 — 66

Names Index

Abrahams, R. G.	58
Augustine, Archbishop of Canterbury	pp101
Barrett, C.K.	127
Barth, K.	115-120
Baxter, R.	109-113
Beattie, J.	102
Bede	101-102
Beesley, P.	102, 107
Bell, G. K.A.	108
Bergman, J.	97
Body, George	73
Boecker, H. J.	59, 60
Brink, L.	99
Clarke, W.K.L.	106
Cornish, F.W.	108
Council of Trent	88
Countryman, L. William	75
Cronzel, H.	100
Dunn, J.D.G.	66
Erasmus	48
Galton and Simpson	50
Gibran, K	145
Gillick, Victoria	15
Goody, J.	101-105
Gorham, C.G.	152
Green, M	54
Hardwicke, Lord	88-89
Harrison, C.	65
Henry VIII	100

Herbert, G	151
Home Office	45
Honecker, M.	120
Huxley, A	120
James, M.R.	98
Knobloch, F.W.	60
Kynaston, David	78
Lake, Catherine	73
Lewis, B	171
Luther, M.	107
Milton, J	139
Morecambe and Wise	50
O'Brien, Cardinal K.	47
Otto, E.	64
Phillpotts, H. Bishop of Exeter	152
Plato and Aristotle	pp82
Poole, Gavin	77
Poole, Matthew	55
Pope Gregory I	101-103
Prince of Wales & Duchess of Cornwall	171
Procter, F. and Frere, W.H.	107
Queen Victoria	108
Quick, O. C.	154-155
Robertson, F.W.	153-154
Rogerson, J and Davies, P	102
Rogerson, J.W.	63, 68, 109, 124
Rousselle, A.	98
Saint Mellion, Cornwall	73
Stevenson, J.	67
Strack, H. L. Billerbeck, P.	61-62
Thane, Pat	86
Thompson, Flora	77
Toynbee, Polly	77
UKHL 12	91
Wilde, O	160
Wills, Martin	73

Subject Index

Acts of Paul and Thecla	98
Adoption	26, 101, 103
Adoption in the Bible	59-60
Adoption law	24
Alternative Service Book (1980)	76 note, 137, 143
Asceticism	97-8
Baptism	105, 142-3, 149-163
Birth certificates	26
Birth of Jesus	60-1
Book of Common Prayer (1549, 1552)	106, 138
Book of Common Prayer (1662)	75-6, 84, 105, 106, 138, 141
Celibacy	84, 100
Centre for Social Justice	77
Children Act 1989	11-14, 16, 19-20, 22, 27, 92
'Christian family', the	79-80, 93
Church of England Synod	139, 168
Churching of women	137-140
Civil Partnership Act 2004	23, 41-3
Civil partnership, dissolution	44-5
Civil partners	24, 31-36, 43-5,
Cohabiting couples	45
'Common law marriages'	88
Common Worship	137, 143, 144, 146
Concubines	56note,

	101, 103, 104
Confirmation	196
Contact	13, 17, 21
Cousin marriage	101, 102, 104
Creation ordinances	54
Deceased wife's sister marriage	108
Divorce	16, 19-20, 42-3, 84,
Families in English law	74-6
Family relationships	128-9
Family structures in the Bible	62-67, 96-7, 123
'Family values'	77
Family, historical perspective	81-90
'Father's Day'	166
Fathers 4 Justice	17
Foster parents	38-9
Gay civil partners	33
'Gay marriage'	48
Godparents	105
Gorham controversy	152-3
Grandparents	39
Guardians	38
Holy Family	93
Household 'codes'	66-7, 98
Human Fertilisation and Embryology Act 2008	23-4
Human Fertilisation and Embryology Authority	31
Human Rights Act	23, 91
Inheritance	27
Illegitimacy statistics	85-6
Jesus, view of family	65-6, 83, 96
Jesus, surrogate birth of	60

Jesus, teaching on divorce	50, 54, 99
Lesbian civil partners	32
Levirate marriage	54, 58-9, 100, 101, 103
Liturgy and liturgies	135-7,
Married heterosexual couples	30-1,
Marriage	41-2, 45, 47-51
Marriage, biblical teaching on	99-100
Marriage Act 1753	88-90
Marriage Act 1836	90 note
Marriage: form versus content	112-120, 123
Marriage : prohibited degrees	107
Marriage: same-sex couples	45-7,
Marriage services	168-70
Methodist Service Book (1999)	142
Monastic life	100, 104
Monogamy	61-2
Mothering Sunday	165-6
Mothers and parental responsibility	30
Naming Ceremonies	147-8, 160-1
New Zealand Prayer Book (1989)	144-6
'No order' principle	18
Parental Order	26
Parental responsibility	13-14, 16, 26, 28-40
Parental rights and duties	14-15
Parents, ways of becoming	25
Parenting	128-132
Parenting in Baptism service	161-2
Paul (Apostle) on marriage	49-50, 97, 99
Paul's 'informal family'	65
Parenting in the Bible	68-7

Polygamy in the Bible	55-7,
Pre-marital intercourse	86-7
Residence	13
Same-sex partnerships	23
Services after a Civil Marriage	171-2
Single parents	36-7
Sororate marriage	55
Step relationships	37-8
Structures of grace	124-6
Surrogacy	24, 26 note, 120
Surrogacy in the Bible	54, 57-8, 140, 142, 146
Thanksgiving for birth of child	
Thanksgiving for gift of a child	141
Unmarried gay couples	36
Unmarried hetero-sexual couples	33-5
Unmarried lesbian couples	35-6
Welfare checklist	16-17